# · The ·
# CURIOUS
## HISTORY
### of the
# RIDDLE

# *The* CURIOUS HISTORY *of the* RIDDLE

SOLVE OVER 250 RIDDLES,

FROM THE RIDDLE OF THE SPHINX

TO HARRY POTTER

*Marcel Danesi, PhD*

WELLFLEET
PRESS

First published in 2020 by Wellfleet Press, an imprint of The Quarto Group, 142 West 36th Street, 4th Floor, New York, NY 10018, USA
T (212) 779-4972 F (212) 779-6058 www.QuartoKnows.com

Wellfleet titles are also available at discount for retail, wholesale, promotional and bulk purchase. For details, contact the Special Sales Manager by email at specialsales@quarto.com or by mail at The Quarto Group, Attn: Special Sales Manager, 100 Cummings Center Suite, 265D, Beverly, MA 01915, USA.

10 9 8 7 6 5 4 3 2 1

ISBN: 978-1-57715-198-2

Library of Congress Cataloging-in-Publication Data

Names: Danesi, Marcel, 1946- author.
Title: The curious history of the riddle : thousands of years of
    conundrums, from the riddle of the Sphinx to Harry Potter / Marcel
    Danesi.
Description: New York : Wellfleet Press, 2020. | Series: Puzzlecraft |
    Includes bibliographical references and index. | Summary: "From the
    first known riddle to the riddles in today's pop culture, The Curious
    History of the Riddle provides a comprehensive investigation of the
    riddle and its origins-plus over 200 riddles to solve"-- Provided by
    publisher.
Identifiers: LCCN 2019052110 (print) | LCCN 2019052111 (ebook) | ISBN
    9781577151982 (paperback) | ISBN 9780760367322 (ebook)
Subjects: LCSH: Riddles--History and criticism. | Riddles in literature.
Classification: LCC PN6367 .D36 2020 (print) | LCC PN6367 (ebook) | DDC
    398.6--dc23
LC record available at https://lccn.loc.gov/2019052110
LC ebook record available at https://lccn.loc.gov/2019052111

Publisher: Rage Kindelsperger • Creative Director: Laura Drew
Managing Editor: Cara Donaldson • Senior Editor: Erin Canning
Cover and Interior Design: Beth Middleworth

Printed in China 1010032020

To my grandchildren,

Alexander, Sarah, and Charlotte.

Their existence has solved the riddle

of my own existence.

# Contents

# INTRODUCTION

*"Let us consider that we are all partially insane. It will explain us to each other; it will unriddle many riddles; it will make clear and simple many things which are involved in haunting and harassing difficulties and obscurities now."*

—MARK TWAIN (1835–1910)

**1.** I AM NEITHER CLOTHES NOR SHOES, YET I CAN BE WORN AND TAKEN OFF, DISAPPEARING. WHAT AM I?

Welcome to the art of riddling. As familiar as a riddle such as this one might appear, it is something that is difficult to explain, and yet we react to it instinctively, searching for an answer that seems to be elusive or impossible at first.

Amazingly, this penchant for riddles is not a learned behavior; it comes naturally in childhood the instant we learn to speak. Like the acquisition of language itself, it comes spontaneously. Children haven't been taught what a riddle is. They simply respond to a riddle and feel compelled to seek an answer.

Even in adulthood, we can't let go of a riddle until we unravel the answer it hides, no matter how dubious or foolish it may be. In case you haven't figured it out, the answer to the riddle opposite is "a smile." In English, a smile is said to be something that, like clothing, can be worn and taken off; therefore, we say things like "wearing a smile," "taking a smile off one's face," and so on. Of course, when a smile is removed, "it disappears from sight."

The riddle itself reveals how we make sense of things by using metaphor and analogy to establish intrinsic connections. In other words, we don't process the world as disconnected elements, but tend to have a more holistic view and look for patterns to process information. Riddles also convey that everything in the world is mysterious until we grasp it on our own terms. And like any mystery, a riddle does indeed leave us in suspense until the flash of insight comes that reveals the truth of the matter. The American writer Henry David Thoreau (1817–1862) once said that for some truly strange reason, human beings see the things of the world as mysterious and feel suspense until their raison d'être is deciphered. Riddles are products of this innate sense of mystery, impelling us to seek out the nature of things by asking questions about them. Thoreau shared his insight into the topic of riddles in *The Maine Woods*, originally published in 1836, when he said, "Talk of mysteries! Think of our life in nature,—daily to be shown matter, to come in contact with it,—rocks, trees, wind on our cheeks! The *solid* earth! The *actual* world! *The common sense! Contact! Contact! Who* are we? *where are we?*"

The riddle is a mini mystery that reverberates with mysticism right below the surface of the language in which it is presented. Its origins and functions go back to the dawn of human civilization. Riddles come in all languages and from all eras of human history, making it a truly "curious" history. This book is about that history. I've taken bits and pieces of information about riddles throughout the ages and weaved them into a tale that is very curious indeed. Riddles originated in the same time frame as the earliest myths. They emerged during the same time frame as the ancient stories of gods and legendary heroes.

One of the first riddles that has come down to us is about one such hero, Oedipus the King, whose inability to avoid his prophesized destiny revolves around a riddle: the Riddle of the Sphinx. The best-known version of the Oedipus story comes from the ancient Greek drama *Oedipus Rex* by Sophocles (ca. 496–406 BCE). The riddle in the story is a metaphor for how life unfolds—like the

phases of a day. Answering the riddle correctly bore enormous consequences, as Oedipus certainly found out.

The early stories and myths are themselves riddles, posing questions about the mystery of existence. Plato (ca. 429–347 BCE) believed that these stories served no real purpose, arising simply out of superstitious traditions that, he asserted, put obstacles along the path of true knowledge. After observing the method of philosophical inquiry of his own teacher, the Athenian philosopher Socrates (ca. 470–399 BCE), whom he greatly admired, Plato proclaimed logic to be the only useful method to gain understanding. But Plato apparently ignored the fact that the central practices of the "superstitious traditions" he denounced were themselves fundamentally inquisitive in the Socratic sense. In fact, riddles mirror Socrates' own method of posing questions in order to arrive at answers that may shed light on the nature of things.

I believe that riddles are small-scale versions of the large-scale questions of existence that philosophers pose. The latter approach rarely produces concrete answers, but riddles do, giving us a sense of relief and satisfaction every time we solve them. The word "catharsis" was used by Aristotle

*OEDIPUS AND THE SPHINX* BY GUSTAVE MOREAU, 1864.

(384–322 BCE) to describe the sense of emotional relief that results from watching a tragic drama on stage, which purges us of pent-up feelings of existential adversity. Unraveling the solution to a riddle seems to produce a similar kind of cathartic effect, albeit in a miniscule way.

The goal of this book is to investigate the fascinating questions about language and human knowledge that the curious history of riddles raises. The greatest puzzle maker of all time, Lewis Carroll—the pseudonym of Charles Dodgson (1832–1898)—viewed riddles as structures born of the imagination. In his two masterpieces of children's literature, *Alice's Adventures in Wonderland* (1865) and *Through the Looking-Glass, and What Alice Found There* (1871), he portrayed the imagination as a region that he called "Wonderland" and "Looking-Glass Land," respectively, inhabited by personified "riddlers," such as Humpty Dumpty, Tweedledee and Tweedledum, the Cheshire Cat, and others. Carroll's imaginary landscapes are where riddles reside. They reveal that we learn about things by wondering about them, no matter how seemingly trivial they are. Alice is always questioning the nature of things, seeking answers in often unusual ways. In the opening chapter of *Alice's Adventures in Wonderland*, she sees a bottle with a label that says, "Drink me!"

Does she drink it or not? It could be poison; after all, humans are natural-born liars and tricksters—and this could be one of their ruses. Alice's response is profoundly Carrollian: "However, this bottle was *not* marked 'poison,' so Alice ventured to taste it, and finding it very nice, (it had, in fact, a sort of mixed flavour of cherry-tart, custard, pine-apple, roast turkey, toffee, and hot buttered toast,) she very soon finished it off."

She answered the riddle by tasting the contents of the bottle. It could have played out much differently, of course. But we accomplish

"DRINK ME!" ILLUSTRATED BY JOHN TENNIEL, FROM *ALICE'S ADVENTURES IN WONDERLAND*.

## WHAT TO EXPECT AND NOT EXPECT

This book does not cover an extensive historiography of riddles. There are several excellent scholarly books that deal with riddles in this way. For example, Eleanor Cook's *Enigmas and Riddles* (2009) is a comprehensive treatment of riddling in literature and culture. Other books of this kind can be found in the notes and bibliography sections at the end of this book. This book does provide a hands-on history of riddles, exemplifying their different forms and functions according to the era in which they emerged. You will get your feet wet (pardon my metaphor) in the river of riddles that has been flowing since the start of time (again, pardon my metaphor) by solving riddles at the end of each chapter.

The ancients saw riddling as a secret prophetic language that required decipherment by gifted or anointed individuals. This explains why the Greek oracles, or ancient fortune-tellers, expressed their divinations in the form of riddles. The underlying belief was that only those who could penetrate the language of riddles would be able to unravel the messages that the gods would send to mortals.

However, not all riddling was believed to have mythic functions; it also served recreational and folkloristic functions from the beginning of time. This can be seen in celebrations, such as the ancient Roman Saturnalia during the month of December, when riddles were created on the spot for guests' enjoyment. Riddles thus reveal the dual nature of humanity, showing us how its two sides are constantly

nothing by doing nothing. Risk is always present in anything we do. We must enter the rabbit hole into which Alice descended to find out what things are all about. The riddle represents the kind of language Alice will find inside the rabbit hole.

My own fascination with riddles started in childhood. I would often become obsessed with finding the answer to a riddle I came across in a children's magazine. As a young man, I read the late Martin Gardner's monthly puzzle column in *Scientific American* with fervor, following up in my local library the enticing historical "leads" that Gardner would provide, and finding, to my constant surprise, that a classic puzzle generally originated in the context of some ancient mythical tradition. Writing this book has itself been akin to solving a riddle, for I had to bring together many textual sources, tidbits of information scattered here and there, and then attempt to discern a general pattern. The search for the latter has been truly revelatory and gratifying. I hope to impart some of the pleasure that investigating riddles has accorded me.

in communication with each other—the sacred and the profane, the mystical and the trivial, the serious and the comedic.

Starting in the medieval period, riddles were composed as miniature poems about common things, such as storms, ships, beer, books, and falcons. What makes these riddles so irresistible is the double-entendre ruse that they embody, highlighting human cleverness. This era documents the birth and rise of riddles as a literary genre all its own—a genre that is still thriving today.

It would take a multi-volume encyclopedia to cover everything there is to know about riddles. Seeing as no one book can cover the history of riddling in any comprehensive way, *The Curious History of the Riddle* offers a concise snapshot of riddles throughout time and what they say about the people and culture surrounding them.

period, though I have had to be selective—there are simply too many worthy riddles to be included within the limited space of this book. Note that the final chapter differs from this format. It deals with rebuses as visual riddles, thus adding some diversity to the historical paradigm and revealing how puzzles are interconnected to each other in specific ways.

In sum, you'll explore riddles through riddling—essentially building your knowledge of an extraordinary phenomenon of human life and language. The connection between riddles and life may seem bizarre, but as Alice was constantly finding out in Wonderland, this may not be a stretch after all. Indeed, the novel continues to be loved to this day, arguably because of this unconscious connection.

If you are an inveterate puzzle solver, you can aim to solve this book's collection of posers (273 in total). Even if you are familiar with some of the riddles (albeit in different guises), chances are you will still find plenty here to keep you occupied and entertained. Let's get started, shall we?

## EXPLORING THE RIDDLE

As you read about the riddles of specific eras, you will also get the chance to solve some of them (with some of the answers explained in the text and all of the answers at the end of the book). This will give you a taste of the riddles of the

## CHAPTER 1

# THE RIDDLE OF THE SPHINX: ANCIENT RIDDLES

*"The Sphinx-riddle. Solve it, or be torn to bits, is the decree."* —D. H. LAWRENCE (1885–1930)

In the city of Giza in Egypt, the massive sculpture known as the Great Sphinx is an awe-inspiring sight that attracts countless visitors every year. It represents a mythic creature with the head of a human and the body of a lion. Dating from before 2500 BCE, the Great Sphinx is 240 feet (73 meters) wide, 66 feet (20 meters) tall, and the width of its face is 13 feet, 8 inches (4.17 meters).

THE GREAT SPHINX IN EGYPT.

Legend has it that a similarly enormous Sphinx guarded the entrance to the ancient city of Thebes. One of the first recorded riddles of human history comes out of that legend. The Riddle of the Sphinx, as it is known, constitutes not only the point of departure for this book, but also the starting point for any study of the relationship among riddle, language, and life. In its basic structure, the Riddle of the Sphinx is a model of what riddles are about—a verbal text that verges toward metaphor and thus never really tells us the direct truth, except through analogy and allusion. Riddles are so common that we hardly ever reflect upon their origin; their appeal is ageless and timeless. When children are posed a riddle such as "Why did the chicken cross the road?" they seek an answer without hesitation, as if impelled by an unconscious instinct to do so.

According to some historians, the Sphinx's riddle comes from the Oedipus legend. When the mythic hero Oedipus approached the city of Thebes, he encountered a gigantic Sphinx guarding the city's entrance. The menacing beast confronted the hero and posed the following riddle to him, warning him that if he failed to answer it correctly, he would die instantly at its hands:

**2. WHAT CREATURE WALKS ON ALL FOURS AT DAWN, TWO AT MIDDAY, AND THREE AT TWILIGHT?**

The fearless Oedipus answered: "Humans, who crawl on all fours as babies, then walk on two legs as grown-ups, and finally need a cane in old age to get around." Upon hearing the correct answer, the astonished Sphinx killed itself, throwing itself off a high rock or devouring itself, depending on the version of the legend. After the Sphinx's death, Oedipus entered Thebes as a hero for destroying the terrible monster that had kept the city in captivity for so long.

Different versions of the riddle exist. The previous one is adapted from the play *Oedipus Rex* by the Greek dramatist Sophocles. Below is a slight variation of the riddle, also dating back to antiquity:

**3. WHAT IS THAT HAS ONE VOICE AND YET BECOMES FOUR-FOOTED, THEN TWO-FOOTED, AND FINALLY THREE-FOOTED?**

Regardless of the version, the Riddle of the Sphinx is one of the oldest, if not the oldest, riddles known. It is more than simple mind-play; it harbors a rather perceptive message by analogy—namely, that the three phases of life (infancy, adulthood, and old age) are comparable respectively to the three phases of a day (morning, noon, and night).

Furthermore, this riddle's function in the Oedipus story suggests that riddles may have

# A Curious Thing

In Greek mythology, the oracle (prophet) at Delphi warned King Laius of Thebes that a son born to his wife, Queen Jocasta, would grow up to kill him and marry her. So, after Jocasta gave birth to a son, Laius ordered that the baby be taken to a mountain and left there to die. As fate would have it, a shepherd rescued the child and brought him to King Polybus of Corinth, who adopted the boy and named him Oedipus.

Oedipus learned about the ominous prophecy during his youth. Believing that Polybus was his real father, he fled to Thebes, of all places, to avoid the prophecy. On the road, he quarreled with a strange man and ended up killing him. At the entrance to Thebes, Oedipus was stopped by an enormous Sphinx, who vowed to kill him if he could not solve its riddle. Oedipus solved it, and as a consequence, the Sphinx took its own life.

In appreciation of ridding them of the monster, the Thebans asked Oedipus to replace King Laius, who had been killed in a duel. He accepted and married Jocasta, the widowed queen.

Several years later, a plague struck Thebes. An oracle said it would end when King Laius' murderer had been driven from Thebes. Oedipus investigated the murder, discovering that Laius was the man he had killed on his way to Thebes. To his horror, he learned that Laius was his real father and Jocasta his mother. In despair, Oedipus blinded himself. Jocasta hanged herself. Oedipus was then banished from Thebes. The prophecy pronounced at Delphi had come true.

A MANUSCRIPT OF SOPHOCLES' *OEDIPUS REX* DATING TO 1340.

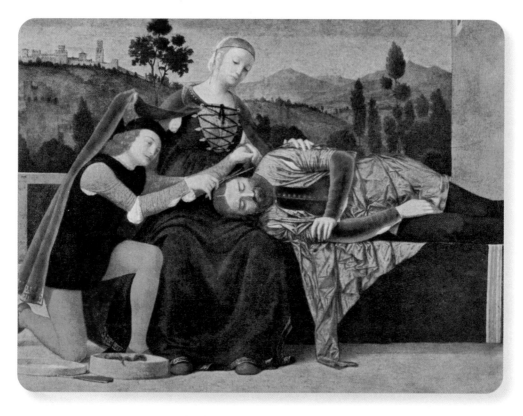

## A Curious Thing

Samson was a judge of ancient Israel, who probably lived in the eleventh century BCE (Judges 13–16). He was renowned for his superhuman strength. He fell passionately for the beautiful Delilah, confiding in her that his strength lay in his long hair, a secret that she discovered by goading Samson into revealing it. She had a servant cut off his hair as he slept, allowing the Philistines to capture Samson, blinding him. But after his hair grew back, he became enraged. Using his re-found strength, he pulled down the pillars of a house, destroying a large group of Philistines and killing himself in the process.

*SAMSON AND DELILAH* BY FRANCESCO MORONE, CA. 1500–1510.

originated as tests of intelligence—more specifically, as indicators of human intelligence and mettle. The biblical story of Samson is further proof of this. At his wedding feast, Samson posed the following riddle to his Philistine guests, whom he mistrusted (Judges 14:14):

**4. OUT OF THE EATER CAME FORTH MEAT, AND OUT OF THE STRONG CAME FORTH SWEETNESS.**

Samson gave the Philistines seven days to come up with the answer, convinced that they would be incapable of doing so. Samson's wife was the only person who knew the answer, and the deceitful guests took advantage of the time they had to coerce the answer from her. When they gave Samson the correct response, the mighty hero became enraged, declaring war against all Philistines.

Enter Delilah, whom Samson loved and who knew the secret of his strength: his long hair. The Philistines bribed Delilah to reveal the secret. So, while Samson was sleeping, she had his hair cut by a servant, and this allowed the Philistines to capture and blind him. But when his hair eventually grew back, Samson acted out his vengeance by knocking down the pillars of a home, killing a large assembly of Philistines and himself as the walls came tumbling down.

All this war and destruction came about due to a simple riddle, which was meant to describe Samson's story of bravery. He had killed a young lion with his bare hands, and then noticed bees constructing a hive in the corpse after returning to it later. The lion is both "the eater" and "the strong"; the "sweetness" refers to the honey that the bees were producing inside the lion's body.

The ancients not only saw riddles as tests of intelligence and moral fortitude, but also as bearing dire consequences for the inability to solve them, as the legends surrounding the Riddle of the Sphinx and the Riddle of Samson attest. The Sphinx devoured anyone who dared to enter the city of Thebes and couldn't answer the riddle. Oedipus did so, and we know what happened to him. Samson's life similarly ended in calamity over a riddle he posed to the Philistines. Legend also has it that the death of the epic poet Homer (ca. 850 BCE) may have been precipitated by the distress he felt at his failure to solve the following riddle, posed to him by a group of fishermen, or according to Heraclitus (ca. 500 BCE), by children, an anecdote also reported by Hesiod (ca. 700 BCE). As in the case of Oedipus, an oracle had predicted that Homer would die because of his inability to solve the following riddle:

**5. WHAT WE CAUGHT, WE THREW AWAY. WHAT WE COULD NOT CATCH, WE KEPT.**

However, not all ancient riddles were devised to test the acumen of mythic heroes or as self-fulfilling prophecies. For example, the biblical kings Solomon and Hiram of Syria sent each other riddles for the pure pleasure of outwitting one another. It was agreed that the unsuccessful competitor would pay a large sum of money to his rival. It appears that Hiram lost a significant amount of money. The ancient Romans made riddling a recreational activity during the Saturnalia, a religious event they celebrated from December 17 to 23. By the fourth century CE, riddles had, in fact, become so popular for their "recreational value" that memory of their mythic origin started to fade.

The Riddle of the Sphinx reflects the prophetic-divinatory function of riddles. Although Sophocles' version is the one most cited, the play *Oedipus and the Sphinx* by Epicharmus of Kos, who is thought to have lived between 550 and 460 BCE, contains one of the first written references to the riddle. According to one myth, the Sphinx was sent by Hera, the sister and wife of Zeus, from Ethiopia to Thebes in Greece. A few accounts suggest that the Sphinx may have uttered a second riddle:

**6. THERE ARE TWO SISTERS: ONE GIVES BIRTH TO THE OTHER AND SHE THEN GIVES BIRTH TO THE FIRST.**

The story of Oedipus has inspired an infinitude of writers, philosophers, artists, and scholars. In the French artist and writer Jean Cocteau's (1899–1963) *The Infernal Machine* (1932), the Sphinx gives the answer of her riddle to Oedipus so that the creature can be freed from killing others and itself, eventually returning to the heavens from where the creature came. In his 1617 book, *Atalanta Fugiens*, which is an eclectic collection of verse, prose, and enigmas of various kinds, German alchemist and physician Michael Maier (1568–1622) claims that the solution to the Sphinx's riddle is the philosopher's stone, the legendary substance for achieving immortality. His reasoning is convoluted, but it revolves around the belief of alchemists that the riddle alludes to the triangle of body, soul, and spirit, which is reflected in the stone. Presumably, the child at the dawn of life mainly perceives the world through the body, while the adult uses the soul to understand things, and in old age, we rely on the spirit to guide us.

The psychoanalyst Sigmund Freud (1856–1939) saw an implicit psychological theory of childhood development in the Oedipus myth. Freud believed that all children exhibit a hostility toward the parent of the same sex and an attraction to the parent of the opposite sex; this attraction eventually manifests itself in some form of neurotic behavior. He wrote about his notion in a letter to a friend: "I have found love of the mother and jealousy of the father in my own case too, and now believe it to be a general phenomenon of early childhood.... If that is the case, the gripping power of *Oedipus Rex*, despite the rational objections to the inexorable fate that the story presupposes, becomes intelligible." [1]

Ancient riddles may have also been used to educate children and encourage literacy in a playful way. A riddle found inscribed on a clay tablet dating back to Babylonian times—around 2000 BCE—is an example of one such riddle. In fact, according to riddle historian Archer Taylor, (1890–1973), "The oldest recorded riddles are

Babylonian school texts . . . from oral tradition that a teacher has put into a schoolbook." [2] Taylor provides some riddles that have unclear answers:

**7. My knees hasten, my feet do not rest, a shepherd without pity drives me to pasture.**

**8. You went and took the enemy's property; the enemy came and took your property.**

**9. Who becomes pregnant without conceiving, who becomes fat without eating?**

Some of the oldest surviving riddles are in the Sanskrit *Rigveda* (between 1500 and 1200 BCE) and various other ancient texts written in the Vedic language, which is a form of Sanskrit. The answers are not given, implying that the solver should search for the spiritual answer they embody. Here is a famous example from the *Rigveda*:

**10. Four are his horns, three are the feet that bear him; his heads are two, his hands are seven in number. Bound with a triple bond the steer roars loudly; the mighty god hath entered into mortals.**

There is no known or singular answer to this riddle, although the allusion to some divinity is clearly implied.

Riddles emerge as part of oral traditions, likely spoken by wise elders in early societies or by teachers aiming to impart wisdom to school children (as the Babylonian tablet seems to imply). With the advent of writing, many of the riddles that became part of cultural folklore were written down, but even so, it was more likely that they were orated or told at gatherings because of low literacy rates. The difference between a riddle as told by an oracle and one by an orator is found in its social function: the former was intended as a cautionary, divinatory, or wise tale, and the latter to entertain people in clever and ingenious ways.

As part of divinatory speech, the Greeks considered riddles to be a product of what they

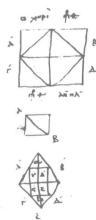

A TENTH CENTURY MANUSCRIPT PAGE FROM PLATO'S *MENO.*

## A Curious Thing

A large body of ancient Hindu texts is called the Vedas, of which there are four main ones. They were composed in a version of ancient Sanskrit and constitute one of the earliest examples of the scripture and literature of Hinduism. The *Rigveda* is one of the four Vedas, constituting a collection of hymns of great literary value. These inspired the composer Gustav Holst (1874–1934) to compose his *Choral Hymns from the Rig Veda* (1907–1908).

**A PAGE FROM THE *RIGVEDA*, CA. 1500–1200 BCE.**

called "mythos," a form of thinking based on belief rather than facts. In contrast, they used "lógos" to designate the kind of thinking used to solve problems in geometry and to logically analyze facts. Aristotle coined the term "mythos" to describe the plot structure of tragedies. Mythos was thus conceived as the form of speech used for poetry, dramatic narratives, and riddles, and lógos, for logical arguments, philosophy, and mathematics. Socrates believed that lógos was innate in all human beings and could be awakened through conscious reflection. In a Socratic dialogue written by Plato, called *Meno* (ca. 385 BCE), Socrates leads an untutored slave to successfully grasp a complicated geometrical problem by getting him to reflect upon the truths of lógos hidden within him through a series of questions he had designed to elicit specific answers. Incidentally, Plato observed in his *Republic* (375 BCE) and *Letters* (360 BCE) (Book II) that riddles have a pedagogical function, supporting their use for children so that they could become aware that certain ideas cannot be formulated logically, requiring mythic speech instead.

The number of historical anecdotes in which ancient riddles play a part is quite large. According to biblical accounts, the Queen of Sheba traveled to Jerusalem to test the famed intellect and wisdom of the great King Solomon with riddles (Kings 10:1–3, Chronicles 9:1–12). Although the actual riddles are not given in the biblical account of her visit, a number that are ascribed to her can be found in the *Midrash Mishlei* (*Midrash on Proverbs*), written in

the medieval period.[3] Other medieval sources also refer to the queen's riddles. Here are a few medieval riddles:

**11. WHAT DOES IT SIGNIFY? A WOMAN SAYS TO HER SON, "YOUR FATHER IS MY FATHER; YOUR GRANDFATHER IS MY HUSBAND; YOU ARE MY SON, AND I AM YOUR SISTER."**

**12. LIVING, MOVES NOT, YET WHEN ITS HEAD IS CUT OFF, IT MOVES.**

**13. WHAT WAS THAT WHICH IS PRODUCED FROM THE GROUND, YET PRODUCES IT, WHILE ITS FOOD IS THE FRUIT OF THE GROUND?**

Riddles are uncommon in the Bible and in Midrashic literature; however, they are found scattered in various Hebrew traditions. The Talmud contains several riddles, such as the following one:

**14. WHAT ANIMAL HAS ONE VOICE LIVING AND SEVEN VOICES DEAD?**

So, what is a riddle? The riddle that the legendary Sphinx asked Oedipus seems to defy an answer at first. What bizarre creature could possibly have four, then two, and finally three limbs, in that order? Wresting an answer from the riddle requires us to think metaphorically, not literally. Metaphor is imprinted in most riddles, from antiquity onward. Their appeal lies in the fact that a figurative twist is built directly into the language, which seems, invariably, to deny words their literal meanings. Not all riddles work in this way, of course. Some play on the facts, laying them out in a certain way that leads us astray. These riddles warn us about taking things at face value. Overall, riddles force us to focus on the nature of language itself and what it allows us to do.

Of course, not all riddles harbor deep messages; some evoke humor. Take, for example, the classic children's riddle "Why did the chicken cross the road?"—the number of answers to this

*TWO RIDDLES OF THE QUEEN OF SHEBA*, A TAPESTRY FROM THE UPPER RHENISH REGION, CA. 1490–1500.

riddle is endless. Here are three possible ones: "To get to the other side," "Because it was taken across by a farmer," and "Because a fox was chasing it."

All three tend to evoke moderate laughter, similar to the response to a punch line of a joke. Many more answers can, of course, be envisioned. Riddles of this kind abound, revealing that they have a lot in common with humor. In fact, this type of riddle is now called a "riddle joke" or "conundrum."

As David Wells points out in his book *The Penguin Book of Curious and Interesting Puzzles*, unlike logic puzzles, where twists or traps might hover fiendishly below the surface of the language in which they are framed, the appeal of riddles lies in the fact that the twist is built directly into the language itself.[4] As we have seen, this invariably denies words their literal meanings. Wells explains, "To the riddle, 'What is the difference between a hill and a pill?' the response, 'One is smaller than the other,' is felt as not being acceptable. The correct answer, recognizable by its twist, is 'One is harder to get up, the other is hard to get down.'"[5] This type of riddle is sometimes called an "abstract riddle," since it doesn't refer to the referent in any direct way, but rather in an abstract way, which allows for many potential answers. The key to solving such riddles lies, as Wells aptly explains, in detecting the artifice with which they are framed.[6] As Helene Hovanec states in her delectable book *The Puzzler's Paradise*, the lure of this genre of riddles lies in the fact that they "simultaneously conceal the answers yet cry out to be solved," piquing solvers to pit "their own ingenuity against that of the constructors."[7]

Overall, a riddle can be defined as an ingenious play on the meanings of words and their combinations. The word derives from Old English *rædels*, meaning "opinion" and "read." As far as can be told, languages of the world have lexical equivalents: in Italian it is *indovinello*, in Croatian *zagonetka*, in Finnish *arvoitus*, in Turkish *bilmece*, and so on. In ancient Greek, the word for "riddle" is *aenigma* (enigma), which meant, rather appropriately, "obscure speech," perfectly describing riddles. The Greeks also used the word *griphos*, which meant "a humorous question with a nonobvious answer," thus distinguishing between abstract riddles and riddle jokes as they are now called. The answer to the riddle "Where does an elephant go when he wants to lie down?" is "Anywhere it pleases." As a riddle joke, it is both humorous and surprising because the question seems to concern the habits of elephants, but it is really about the intimidating size of elephants.

All riddles, whether divinatory, abstract, recreational, pedagogical, or humorous, impart an unconscious feeling that words are magical. To quote Freud from *Introductory Lectures on Psychoanalysis* (1917), "Words and magic were in the beginning one and the same thing, and even today words retain much of their magical power." The source of magic is likely to be the operation of metaphor. It was the Greek philosopher Aristotle who coined the term "metaphor" (*metapherein* means "to transfer") in *Poetics* and *Rhetoric* (both ca. fourth century BCE) to explain how language creates infinite meanings with a limited set of resources, suggesting that metaphor and riddles are often one and the same. To see the connection between the two, consider the following riddle:

**15. IT CAN BE DONE IN SOMEONE'S FACE OR OUT OF THE OTHER SIDE OF YOUR MOUTH, BUT IT IS NEITHER SPIT NOR KISSING. WHAT IS IT?**

The meanings of "laugh," the answer to this riddle, are metaphorical, as in "laugh in someone's face" (to show contempt for someone) and "laugh out of the other side of one's mouth" (to feel embarrassed after realizing one is wrong in feeling satisfaction about something). These are the meanings built into the above riddle.

It should be noted that Aristotle defined both metaphor and riddles as "proportions of thought." For example, in the metaphor "Old age is the evening of life," an equality can be set up as follows: A = old age, B = life, C = evening, D = day; therefore, A is to B as C is to D. The reasoning involved can be broken down as follows: the period of childhood is to life as the morning is to the day; the period of adulthood is to life as the afternoon is to the day; hence, old age is to life as the evening is to the day. This logic is Aristotle's interpretive key to decoding the Riddle of the Sphinx. He states, "The very nature indeed of a riddle is this, to describe a fact in an impossible combination of words (which cannot be done with the real names of things, but can be with their metaphorical substitutes) . . . because the hearer expected something different, his acquisition of the new idea impresses him all the more." [8]

In sum, most riddles involve a metaphorical play on words that seems to reveal something that may not have been obvious. They may also be based on double entendre—a play on the double meanings of a word or phrase—so as to force us to focus on the different meanings of words. For example, the word "play" can refer to engagement in physical activities for enjoyment, as in "We play baseball every once in a while," or to a theatrical work, as in "I love the plays of Chekhov." This double entendre can be translated into the form of a riddle as follows:

**16. IT IS SOMETHING THEATRICAL AND ALSO PHYSICAL. WHAT IS IT?**

The first riddles originated at around the same time as the first civilizations. The themes they espoused had an archetypal sense to them, dealing with a common understanding of the world throughout antiquity. For example, the Riddle of the Sphinx's "phases of life" theme is found across ancient societies.

An archetype theory of the origins of riddles implies that they emanate from a shared experience of reality that is lodged in the collective unconscious of humanity. The fact that similar and even identical riddle traditions exist across the world and across cultures, regardless of language, suggests

# A Curious Thing

The term "archetype," as used in psychology and literary criticism, is an unconscious figure of mind that finds expression in rituals, symbols, forms, and words. Archetypes are deeply rooted in the psyche, deriving from the experience of basic life events. They are understood in the same way across time and geographic space, although their manifestations vary. For example, the Riddle of the Sphinx embodies the archetype of the phases of life. The term used in this way was initiated by Swiss psychologist Carl Jung (1875–1961), who defined it as a mental image inherited from our ancestors as part of a "collective unconscious," containing the feelings and thoughts developed cumulatively by the species that are directive of the human condition. Jung described the unconscious as a "receptacle" of primordial images shared by all humanity that have become such an intrinsic part of everyday life as to be beyond reflection.

A HAND-DRAWN PORTRAIT OF CARL JUNG.

that their metaphorical structure is intrinsic to human consciousness. Because there is little or no chance that the people of these cultures were in contact with each other, the implication is that the archetypes found in riddles are indeed universal.

Dutch historian Johan Huizinga characterized the human species as *Homo ludens*, emphasizing the playful, or ludic, element, both physical and intellectual, in the constitution of early cultures and thus in the origins of human consciousness.[9] At an unconscious level, we still perceive life itself as a kind of existential riddle or game. The use of the word "riddle" in everyday discourse—the riddle of life, the riddle of the universe, the riddle of language, etc.—reverberates with metaphysical overtones to this very day. Riddles thus reveal a universal feature of human thought: our ability to interpret reality, rather than just refer to it. Riddles are early examples of how we conceptualize many abstractions and come to interpret them through metaphorical language. They were, and continue to be, intrinsic components of folk wisdom. In reference to Malaitian riddles, the renowned anthropologist and folklorist Elli Köngäs-Maranda (1932–1982) says, "Riddles make a point of playing with conceptual boundaries and crossing them for the intellectual pleasure of showing that things are not quite as stable as they seem."[10]

POSTER FOR THE OPERA *TURANDOT*, WHICH IS REFERENCED IN RIDDLES 27 TO 29 ON PAGE 31.

# SOLVE THESE ANCIENT AND EARLY RIDDLES

(THE ANSWERS START ON PAGE 124)

**17.** A riddle from ancient Sumer, around four thousand years ago, found on an ancient Sumerian cuneiform tablet: There is a house. One enters it blind and comes out seeing. What is it?

(HINT: THINK OF BLINDNESS AND SIGHT AS METAPHORS.)

**18.** Another ancient Babylonian riddle, believed by some to be one of the oldest riddles of humanity: What becomes pregnant without conceiving and fat without eating?

(HINT: THE ANSWER CONCERNS SOMETHING IN NATURE WE SEE EVERY DAY.)

**19.** A riddle from Estonian mythology, constituting a version of the phases of life myth imprinted in the Riddle of the Sphinx: It goes in the morning on four feet, at lunchtime on two, at evening on three. [11]

**20.** An adaptation of a riddle attributed to the Greek poet Cleobolus, who lived in the sixth century BCE (appears in *The Greek Anthology*, discussed in the next chapter): There is one father and twelve children; of these each has thirty daughters of different appearance. Some are white to look at and the others black in turn. They are immortal and yet they all fade away.

(HINT: AGAIN, THINK METAPHORICALLY, AND CONSIDER ESPECIALLY WHAT THE NUMBERS MIGHT REFER TO. THIS IS A TOUGH ONE THOUGH.)

**21.** A riddle from Norse mythology: King Hiedrek was about to imprison a man named Gestumblindi if he could not come up with riddles that would stump the king. Gestumblindi prayed to the Allfather, who came to his aid, disguising himself as Gestumblindi. The god Odin had prepared him with riddles, which the king answered, including this one: "Four hang, four sprang, two point the way, two to ward off dogs, one dangles after, always rather dirty. What am I?" Eventually, King Heidrek could not answer the riddle. Enraged, the king attacked Odin, causing the god to flee.

(HINT: THINK ANATOMICALLY! THIS IS ANOTHER TOUGH NUT.)

**22.** A riddle that exemplifies a common archetype, which manifested itself across Europe and Asia (this one comes from Sanskrit): It is a twelve-spoked wheel, on which stand 720 sons of one birth. [12]

**23.** A riddle from the Kwa language of Ewe culture, which covers the areas of Ghana, Togo, and Benin: This woman has not been to the riverside for water, but there is water in her tank.

(HINT: IT CAN REFER TO A COMMON FRUIT IN EWE SOCIETY OR A PERSON.)

RIDDLES 24 TO 26 ARE FROM THE ANCIENT SANSKRIT LANGUAGE.[13]

**24**. Who moves in the air?
(HINT: THE "WHO" DOES NOT REFER TO A HUMAN BEING.)

**25**. Who makes a noise on seeing a thief?
(HINT: AGAIN, THE "WHO" DOES NOT REFER TO A HUMAN BEING.)

**26**. Who is the enemy of lotuses?
(HINT: FOR PLANTS, THIS IS A COMMON "ENEMY.")

RIDDLES 27 TO 29 ARE FROM THE OPERA *TURANDOT* (1926) BY GIACOMO PUCCINI (1858–1924), WHICH IS BASED ON A TWELFTH-CENTURY TALE BY THE PERSIAN POET NIZAMI (1141–1209).

**27**. What is born each night and dies at dawn?
(HINT: IT IS NOT THE MOON, BUT SOMETHING THAT EACH SUITOR BEARS.)

**28**. What flickers red and warm like a flame, yet is not fire?
(HINT: AGAIN, THINK METAPHORICALLY. A CLEARER VERSION MAY BE "WHAT LIQUID IS RED AND WARM LIKE FIRE AND FLOWS LIKE WATER?")

**29**. What is like ice yet burns?
(HINT: UNREQUITED LOVE IS INVOLVED IN THIS RIDDLE. TO WHOM MIGHT IT REFER WITHIN THE NARRATIVE?)

**30**. A riddle from Finnish folklore: Bunched up behind the hummock, curled up under a stone, a disc at the foot of a stump.[14]

THE SOURCES OF RIDDLES 31 TO 34 ARE NOT KNOWN FOR CERTAIN; THEY APPEAR IN DIFFERENT GUISES AND LANGUAGES, SO IT CAN BE ASSUMED THAT THEY SPAN TIME AND SPACE CONSIDERABLY. AND EVEN IF THEY TURN OUT NOT TO BE ANCIENT, THEY ARE STILL CLASSIC RIDDLES THAT WILL CHALLENGE YOU TO FIND AN ANSWER.

**31**. They come out at night without being fetched; by day they disappear without being stolen.

**32**. It never was, but always will be. No one has ever seen me, nor ever will. And yet I have the confidence of all that will live and breathe on this terrestrial ball.
(HINT: THIS IS ANOTHER RIDDLE THAT CONCERNS TIME AND HOW WE NAME SEGMENTS OF TIME.)

**33**. It runs but does not walk; it murmurs, but does not talk; it has a bed, but it does not sleep; it has a mouth but does not eat.

**34**. No sooner spoken than it is broken. What is it?

**35**. A riddle from Chinese folklore: Washing makes it more and more dirty; it is cleaner without washing.

**36**. A riddle from Tamil folklore: If the sun sets, it will let you see a flower-garden; but if you look at it after dawn, you will see an empty garden. What is it?

# CHAPTER 2

# EDUCATION AND FAITH: MEDIEVAL RIDDLES

*"We are caught inside a mystery, veiled in an enigma, locked inside a riddle."* —TERENCE MCKENNA (1946–2000)

There is little doubt that riddles were mainly spoken and passed on by word of mouth in antiquity, as people likely posed them at gatherings and celebrations, perhaps to impress listeners. However, some riddles became part of literary traditions early on, as a collection of poetry, riddles, and other literary genres called *The Greek Anthology* implies, which is likely to have been compiled in the medieval period with versions of the manuscript first appearing around 1000 CE. This collection was likely meant to be enjoyable reading. By the early medieval period (ca. 500 CE), riddling started migrating more and more away from the realm of myth to that of literary-aesthetic artistry, as witnessed by the fact that most of the riddles of the era were composed as miniature poems.

One of the first texts that contained a collection of such poetic riddles comes from the fourth or fifth century CE and was written by a certain Symphosius, about whom virtually nothing is known. It is called the *Aenigmata Symphosii* (*The Enigmas of Symphosius*), consisting of one hundred riddles in the form of brief Latin poems called "epigrams." The first edition of the *Aenigmata*, known as the *Editio princeps*, was published in 1533, in Paris, by Joachimus Perionius. But the riddles have come down to us in over thirty manuscripts, the most notable of which is the Codex Salmasianus (ca. seventh or eighth century CE), which is preserved at the French National Library in Paris.

Unlike mythic riddles, such as the Riddle of the Sphinx, Symphosius' collection deals mainly with everyday objects and themes (animals, writing, etc.), rather than existential questions. Here are two examples:[15]

### 37. Unlike my mother, in semblance different; from my father, of mingled race, a breed; unfit for progeny, of others am I born, and; none is born of me.

### 38. Sweet darling of the banks, always close to the depths, sweetly I sing for the Muses; when drenched with black, I am the tongue's messenger by guiding fingers pressed.

The first riddle, about a "mule," is an allusive one, referring to the mule as the offspring of a donkey and a horse (of "mingled race" and "of others am I born") and sterile ("none is born of me"). The second riddle, about a "reed," describes writing, and it is the second riddle in the collection of Symphosius. Reed material for writing was common in the era—it is a plant that grows in water ("sweet darling of the banks"). The riddle alludes to the fact that writing in the era was used mainly for poetry ("I sing for the Muses") and executed with black ink ("drenched with black"). As a substitution of oral speech ("the tongue's messenger"), writing is carried out by "guiding fingers pressed." This riddle shows the growing fascination with writing and literacy that was gaining momentum in the medieval era.

A similar riddle, with the same fascination with writing, is found in ninth-century Italy. It is a brief manuscript, constituting the first written document to show a conscious use of a *volgare* ("a tongue of the people"), rather than Latin; it is a four-line riddle written in early Veronese, and hence it has come to be known as the *Indovinello veronese* (*Veronese Riddle*). The manuscript is preserved in Verona in the Biblioteca Capitolare.

The traditional interpretation of the riddle is that the author is writing with a pen that is "prodding his oxen over white fields" (that is, writing on white paper) as it is "sowing black seed" (ink):

**39. SE PAREVA BOVES**
*HE PRODDED HIS OXEN TO*
*MOVE FORWARD*
**ALBA PRATALIA ARABA**
*PLOWING WHITE FIELDS*
**(ET) ALBO VERSORIO TENEBA**
*AND A WHITE PLOW HE HELD*
**(ET) NEGRO SEMEN SEMINABA.**
*SOWING BLACK SEED.*

Some questions regarding the language of the *Indovinello* have been debated in the relevant literature. For example, some scholars posit that the verb *parere* means "to appear," rather than "to prod oxen to move forward." However, most assign the latter meaning to it because it continues to be a dialectal form used in the region of Verona and it fits in with the overall meaning of the text, which is a typical medieval riddle in which "field," "plow," and "seed" represent aspects of writing metaphorically.

Symphosius himself starts with riddles about the act of writing, indicating that he was likely aware of the growing power of literacy in an age

DEPICTION OF A SYMPOSIUM ON A PIECE OF POTTERY, CA. 420 BCE.

of oral traditions and perhaps wanting it to spread throughout his own society. The riddles are written in an elegant classical Latin grammar and style. In the preface, Symphosius asserts that he wrote them to be used at the festivities during the Roman Saturnalia. Although they were written down, they were still likely meant to be orated. Moreover, they reflect the same type of style and themes of typical Saturnalia riddles (written in tercets of dactylic hexameters) and are similar to the riddles in the *Xenia*, a collection of epigrams composed by Marcus Valerius Martial (40–104 CE), a Roman poet born in Hispania.

As mentioned previously, the Greeks also used riddling at their symposia, or banquets. The riddling used at the banquets might be compared to a quiz game in which the participants could win prizes for solving them correctly. These banquets are described in Plato's *Symposium* and several Greek poems, as well as portrayed in Greek and Etruscan art.

A clue that the riddles may have been meant to be spoken at a symposium is the fact that the answer is written at the start, which is called a *lemma*, suggesting that it was intended to be read out loud by someone who was literate—and knowing the answer, the person would be better able to dramatize the riddle. Many of these riddles are condensed fables, reminiscent of the ancient fables of Aesop (sixth century BCE) and dealing with animals as metaphors for human character. The preface to a subsequent edition of the *Aenigmata* states that "within Symphosius' milieu there is still a conception of riddles as oral and agonistic," supporting the presumption that riddling was part of oral festive competitions.

The so-called *Greek Anthology* is another collection of riddles that surfaced around the same time as the *Aenigmata*. Some historians credit the Greek poet, mathematician, and grammarian Metrodorus (ca. 500 CE) with composing this work. It may, however, have been put together much earlier, even as far back as the seventh century BCE, and may have been the cumulative work of many authors combined into one volume (perhaps by Metrodorus), as indicated by the content of some of the riddles that reach back to antiquity.

Many are truly challenging, requiring rather sophisticated knowledge of Greek mythology and history:[16]

**40. IF YOU PUT ONE HUNDRED IN THE MIDDLE OF A BURNING FIRE, YOU WILL FIND THE SON AND A SLAYER OF A VIRGIN.**

This riddle is solved by combining the Greek symbol for one hundred, *rho*, with the word *pyros*, which means "fire," to make the name/answer "Pyrrhos," the son of Deidamia and the slayer of Polyxena. Solving this riddle requires specific knowledge, because you would have to know how to spell the words it's referring to. This is an example of an "enigma," which is discussed in more detail in chapter 4. By and large, medieval riddles were designed to be interesting,

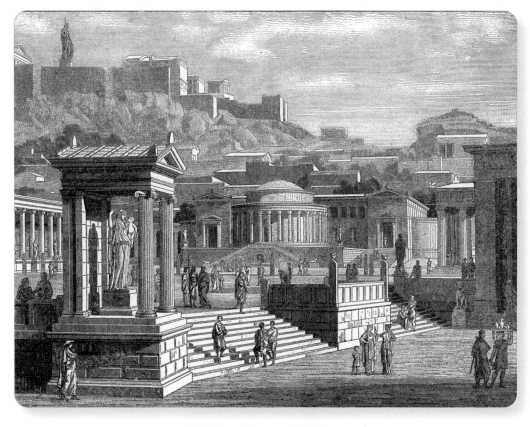

## A Curious Thing

Nothing is known about Symphosius' life. Even his name may not be his real name, but rather a pseudonym meaning "party boy," alluding to the Greek symposium (a banquet with dancing and riddling), both phonetically and referentially. The exact date of his *Aenigmata* is also unknown. Proposed dates have ranged from the third to the fifth century CE. The scholar Erin Sebo presents circumstantial evidence that can be gleaned from the riddles themselves, suggesting that Symphosius wrote them in Latin while living in North Africa or that Symphosius was African himself.[17]

A DEPICTION FROM 1890 OF THE AGORA OF ATHENS IN ANCIENT GREECE.

A FOLIO FROM A LATER DEPICTION OF THE *MAHABHARATA*, CA. 1800–1850.

linguistically and culturally, but they were also created to provide humorous social critique, such as to castigate a dreadful host at a party or to satirically memorialize the dead, alongside sober reflections on life and love.

The medieval period saw a flourishing of riddle collections that became staples of folk culture. The compilers were likely of elite social status, seeing as they were literate and could read them out loud in a dramatic fashion. The great medieval Hindu epic, the *Mahabharata* (ca. 400 CE), which depicts the civil war waged between the five Pandava brothers and their one hundred stepbrothers at Kurukshetra near modern Delhi, also includes riddles and describes riddle contests, not unlike those of ancient Greece and Rome. Many of the text's themes involve philosophical and existential questions, such as the following one posed by a nature spirit to the heroic characters:

### 41. WHAT IS THE HIGHEST REFUGE OF VIRTUE? WHAT OF FAME? WHAT OF HEAVEN? AND WHAT, OF HAPPINESS?

The answer, "liberality," is portrayed in the work as the highest refuge of virtue, a gift of fame, the truth of heaven, and a source of true happiness. The riddles in this work require knowledge of the philosophical tenets of Hinduism, but their answers do embody universal truths.

Symphosius' anthology may have been the source and inspiration for many riddle collections shortly after it became widely known. The one hundred riddles of Aldhelm (640–709 CE), who was a medieval English scholar and poet, the abbot of Malmesbury Abbey, and the bishop of Sherbourne, were inspired by those of Symphosius in style and thematic range. Similarly named *Enigmata*—confirming that "enigma" was the common word for "riddle" in medieval Latin—they were included in a treatise Aldhelm wrote for the king of Northumbria. This became one of the most widely quoted texts of the medieval period—in large part because of the riddles, which were about everyday things, such as animals, plants, and household items, and their social meanings. The following riddles constitute vivid metaphorical portraits of two common medieval referents:

### 42. LONG SINCE, THE HOLY POWER THAT MADE ALL THINGS SO MADE ME THAT MY MASTER'S DANGEROUS FOES I SCATTER. BEARING WEAPONS IN MY JAWS, I SOON DECIDE FIERCE COMBATS; YET I FLEE BEFORE THE LASHINGS OF A LITTLE CHILD.

### 43. I SHARE WITH THE SURF ONE DESTINY IN ROLLING CYCLES WHEN EACH MONTH REPEATS. AS BEAUTY IN MY BRILLIANT FORM RETREATS, SO TOO THE SURGES FADE IN CRESTING SEA.

Aldhelm's riddles constitute a poetic historiography of the era, allowing us to imagine life and things of the period through ingenious metaphorical portrayals. Aldhelm is thought to be the first English scholar to write in Latin. As mentioned, he compiled one hundred riddles that were part of a larger text, *Epistola ad Acircium* (*Letter to Acircius*), a fascinating work itself that includes, among other things, a discussion of the meanings of the number seven and a list of words illustrating the different meters used in writing poetry. The riddles were written in hexameters and may have been added to the *Epistola* to demonstrate the features and aesthetic qualities of this form of poetic meter. The hexameter consists of six poetic feet per verse line; it was the standard form in classical Greek and Latin poetry.

Even though the riddles were written in Latin, Aldhelm's *Enigmata* became part of Anglo-Saxon literary traditions, inspiring similar works in the Anglo-Saxon culture of the era, including the *Enigmata* of Saint Boniface, which were intended to emphasize the importance of Christian virtues to young people. Similarly, Tatwine (ca. 670–734 CE), a Benedictine monk and later the archbishop of Canterbury from 731 to 734 CE, composed forty riddles in the style of Aldhelm to illustrate the importance of objects and ideas in God's scheme of things.

The objective of spreading learning and literacy was adopted a little later by the English scholar Alcuin of York (735–804 CE), also known as Albinus. He is best known for his collection of mathematical and logical puzzles, the *Propositiones ad acuendos juvenes* (*Problems to Train the Young*). Like those before him, he also saw riddles as a source for promoting literacy. He sent the following one to Archbishop Riculf of Mainz, known by the nickname Damoeta, to express gratitude after receiving a gift from him:

44. A BEAST HAS SUDDEN COME TO THIS MY HOUSE. A BEAST OF WONDER, WHO TWO HEADS HAS GOT, AND YET THE BEAST HAS ONLY ONE JAWBONE. TWICE THREE TIMES TEN OF HORRID TEETH IT HAS.

ITS FOOD GROWS ON THIS BODY OF MINE, NOT FLESH, NOR FRUIT. IT EATS NOT WITH ITS TEETH, DRINKS NOT. ITS OPEN MOUTH SHOWS NO DECAY. TELL ME, DAMOETA DEAR, WHAT BEAST IS THIS?

The solution to Alcuin's riddle, "a comb," hinges on decoding the metaphorical meaning of "beast" as a device rather than an animal. As part of the art of correspondence, Alcuin expected a reply in kind, which indicates that literary riddling in the era was part of an emerging cultural tradition of written communication. As medievalist Paul Sorrell aptly points out, this riddle constitutes a perfect example of what a literary riddle is all about: a means of shedding light on and critiquing everyday life, including its trivial objects, using poetic techniques of construction.[18]

Sorrell also notes that the comb was a deluxe one made from elephant ivory, and in 794 CE, it was sent to Alcuin, who used the occasion to create a riddle—transforming the object into an animal, anthropomorphically speaking.[19] Most of Alcuin's riddles are found in the *Disputatio regalis et nobilissimi juvenis Pippini cum Albino scholastico* (*Dialogue of Pepin, the Most Noble and Royal Youth, with the Teacher Albinus*), a document written in the form of a dialogue in which he, Alcuin (also called Albinus), converses with twelve-year-old Pippin, the second son of Charlemagne and one of his pupils. Their conversation involves a Socratic discussion of the nature of abstract ideas. Here is an example:

Always the dedicated teacher, Alcuin is more famous for his collection of mathematical and logical problems, which he designed as a textbook for students to develop their critical thinking skills. Perhaps his most famous puzzle is this one:

**46. A CERTAIN MAN NEEDED TO TAKE A WOLF, A GOAT, AND A HEAD OF CABBAGE ACROSS A RIVER. HOWEVER, HE COULD ONLY FIND A BOAT WHICH WOULD CARRY TWO AT A TIME— HIMSELF AND ONE OTHER. HOW DID HE GET ALL OF THEM ACROSS UNHARMED, SINCE IF LEFT ALONE, THE WOLF WOULD EAT THE GOAT AND THE GOAT WOULD EAT THE CABBAGE?**

First, the man goes across the river with the goat, leaving the wolf and cabbage alone with no dire consequences, seeing as wolves don't eat cabbage. On the other side of the river, he drops off the goat and comes back alone. When he gets back to the original side, he must decide between the wolf or the cabbage. Let's say he goes with the cabbage. He crosses the river with the cabbage, drops it off, and then goes back to the original side with the goat in tow (since the goat would eat the cabbage). Back on the original side, he drops off the goat and goes over to the other side with the wolf. He drops off the wolf with the cabbage and then travels back alone to pick up the goat. He rows to the other side with the

A 1928 STAINED-GLASS RENDERING OF ALDHELM IN MALMESBURY ABBEY, WHERE HE WAS AN ABBOT.

**45. WHAT IS IT THAT MAKES BITTER THINGS SWEET?**

## A Curious Thing

Alcuin of York (735–804 CE), also known as Albinus, was a renowned medieval scholar, teacher, and writer. He studied at the cloister school of York, which was the center of learning in England during his era. Alcuin became an adviser to Emperor Charlemagne in 782. In 796, Charlemagne made him abbot of St. Martin at Tours in France. During this post, Alcuin helped to spread the achievements of Anglo-Saxon scholarship throughout Europe, bringing about the revival of learning known as the Carolingian Renaissance. Alcuin's puzzle anthology became widely known in the medieval world, and many of his puzzles have found their way into contemporary collections. All of them require a high degree of ingenuity to solve, despite their apparent simplicity.

*CHARLEMAGNE RECIEVES ALCUIN, 780* BY JEAN-VICTOR SCHNETZ (1787–1870).

goat, and then collecting all three—the goat, the wolf, and the cabbage—he continues on his journey.

Riddles warn us of the power of language to deceive. So, it comes as little surprise to find that in the tenth century, many famous Arabic scholars used riddles to expose the dangers that figurative language poses in written laws, coinciding with the establishment of the first law schools in Europe. One such riddle master was the Arab poet Al-Hariri of Basra (ca. 1050–1120), whose collection was called *Assemblies*, because riddles and problems of grammar were assembled in one volume. Al-Hariri's riddles illustrate the ambiguities and hidden meanings that metaphors can introduce into discourse, and warn people against them.

As mentioned, the medieval riddles were about everyday things and people, as well as matters of faith and God. They reflect the use of riddles as part of an emerging literary genre. In addition to the riddle art of Symphosius, Aldhelm, and Alcuin, the Exeter Book is a medieval Anglo-Saxon collection of nearly one hundred riddles, dealing with everyday subjects and themes in medieval life. Written anonymously, these riddles are composed as miniature poems about such common things as storms, ships, beer, books, and falcons. The Exeter Book is written in Anglo-Saxon, not Latin. Also known as the Codex Exoniensis, it's the largest known extant collection of Old English literature. Some of the riddles are obvious, but others are extremely difficult to understand. Occasionally, the riddle is phrased suggestively in a prurient sense, as the following one illustrates:

**47. I AM A WONDROUS CREATURE FOR WOMEN IN EXPECTATION, A SERVICE FOR NEIGHBORS. I HARM NONE OF THE CITIZENS EXCEPT MY SLAYER ALONE. MY STEM IS ERECT, I STAND UP IN BED, HAIRY SOMEWHERE DOWN BELOW. A VERY COMELY PEASANT'S DAUGHTER DARES SOMETIMES, PROUD MAIDEN, THAT SHE GRIPS AT ME, ATTACKS ME IN MY REDNESS, PLUNDERS MY HEAD, CONFINES ME IN A STRONGHOLD, FEELS MY ENCOUNTER DIRECTLY, WOMAN WITH BRAIDED HAIR. WET BE THAT EYE.**

The riddle may be seemingly alluding to male genitalia, but the answer is "an onion," which fits in with the riddle's metaphorical description of onions.

This kind of riddling may well have been a way to get around the moralistic strictures and censorship imposed by the Church on language in that era. The sexual double-entendre style of riddling became rather diffuse, as can be seen in the following riddle by a Benedictine Czech monk named Claret (also known as Claretus). He became quite famous by exploiting sexual innuendo, creating quasi-obscene riddles intended presumably as vehicles of prurient entertainment.

His collection was also called *Enigmata*:[20]

**48. A vessel have I. That is round like a pear, Moist in the middle, Surrounded with hair; And often it happens That water flows there.**

Like the riddle in the Exeter Book, the image that the impish monk obviously wanted to elicit in his reader was a transparently sexual one, although the actual answer of "an eye" works as well because it is the result of a double entendre. Incidentally, riddles with the same kind of prurient nuances are found in Aldhelm's *Enigmata*, suggesting that the riddle makers played around with the contrast between the sacred and the profane in a profoundly religious era. This means that most of the riddle books, outside of those by Alcuin and a few others, probably had much more than a simple pedagogical function, but rather a recreational-literary one. However, they also spanned themes of faith, thus combining the sacred and the profane into complementary themes in the era. In effect, worship and laughter went hand in hand via the same literary form of the riddle.

In sum, the art of riddling in the medieval era was, overall, a multifaceted one used for religious purposes, for education, and for laughter. Every object and creature of creation is worthy of the riddler's attention, no matter how profane the topic might be. Even the prurient riddles harbored a religious subtext: do not be led astray by profanity, for it will always dupe you.

## A Curious Thing

The Exeter Book is one of four major examples of medieval Anglo-Saxon literature, along with the Vercelli Book, the Nowell Codex, and the Caedmon Manuscript. It was donated to the library at Exeter in 1072 by Leofric, the first bishop of Exeter, hence its name. It was compiled in the period between 960 to 990 CE. Originally it is believed to have contained 131 leaves, of which 8 are lost. Because the Exeter Book is the largest known extant collection of English literature, UNESCO recognized it as one of the world's principal cultural artifacts.

A SOUTHERN RAILWAY PRINT OF EXETER CATHEDRAL, BY DONALD MAXWELL (1877–1936).

# SOLVE THESE MEDIEVAL RIDDLES

(THE ANSWERS START ON PAGE 126)

RIDDLES 49 TO 54 ARE FROM *AENIGMATA* BY SYMPHOSIUS.

**49**. A modest maid, too well I observe the law of modesty; I am not pert in speech nor rash of tongue; of my own accord I will not speak, but I answer him who speaks. (number 98)

**50**. Great powers from little strength I bring. I open closed houses, but again I close the open. I guard the house for the master, but in turn am guarded by him. (number 4)

**51**. I do not lay claim to strength for my body as a whole, but in a battle of heads I refuse to strive with none; large is my head, my whole weight too therein. (number 86)

**52**. I give vent to hoarse sounds in the water's midst, but my voice with praise resounds, as if it too were sounding its own praises; and though I am ever singing, no one praises my songs. (number 19)

**53**. Small is my body but greater is my wisdom. I am versed in trickery, cunning, keen-witted; and a wise beast am I, if any beast is termed wise. (number 34)

**54**. No fixed form is mine, yet none is stranger to me. My brightness lies within, sparkling with radiant light, which shows nothing except what it has seen before. (number 69)

**55**. A riddle from *The Greek Anthology*: No one who looks sees me, though who does not look sees. Who does not speak, speaks; who does not run, runs. I am a liar and yet I can tell all truth.

**56**. A riddle from the Indian *Mahabharata*: What is man's surest weapon in danger?

RIDDLES 57 TO 63 ARE FROM ALDHELM'S *ENIGMATA*.

**57**. I share with the surf one destiny in rolling cycles when each month repeats. As beauty in my brilliant form retreats, so too the surges fade in cresting sea.

**58**. Formed in a marvelous way, born without seed, I loan my sweet breast with treasure from flowers. By my art the golden platters of kings grow yellow. Always I bear the small, sharp spears of cruel war and though I lack hands, my spear stings more cruelly than weapons forged by smiths.

**59**. I am a faithful, vigilant guardian, always watching the house. In the deep night, I walk through the unseeing shadows for I do not lose the sight of my eyes, even in black caverns. Against the hateful thieves who ravage the stores of grain, I ambush, I silently set a snare of death. A roaming huntress, I invade the lairs of wild beasts. But I do not wish to chase fleeing herds alongside dogs who bark and bring cruel war against me.

**60**. Who would not be amazed by my strange lot? With my strength, I bear a thousand forest oaks. But a slender needle at once pierces me, the bearer of such burdens. Birds flying in the sky and fish swimming in the sea once took their first life from me. A third of the world is held in my power.

**61**. No one can see me or catch me in their palms. I spread the noisy sound of my voice quickly through the world. I can break to pieces the oak with my loud, crashing strength as I beat against the high poles of the sky and traverse the fields.

**62**. From the trunk of a willow and the scraped hide of a cow I am made. Suffering the fierce savagery of war, I with my own body always save my bearer's body, unless death takes the man's life. What fierce soldier endures such a fate or receives so many deadly wounds in war?

**63**. Multicolored in hue, I flee the sky and the deep earth. There is no place for me on the ground nor in any part of the poles. No one fears an exile as cruel as mine. But I make the world grow green with my rainy tears.

RIDDLES 64 AND 65 ARE FROM ALCUIN'S *DISPUTATIO*.

**64**. This is a hunt for something that belongs among peasants. (Hint: This refers to a parasite that lives on the skin that was thought, at the time, to afflict peasants.)

**65**. I saw someone born before he was conceived. You saw this, and perhaps you ate it.

RIDDLES 66 TO 70 ARE FROM THE EXETER BOOK. SINCE THE ANSWERS WERE NOT PROVIDED IN THE BOOK, ONLY INFERENCES CAN BE MADE, SO THERE MAY BE OTHER ANSWERS THAN THE ONES PROVIDED IN THIS BOOK FOR THESE RIDDLES.

**66**. How many men are clever enough to identify who sends me on my journey? I go, brave and roaring across the earth, burning buildings and houses in my wake. Smoke rises from the fires as I leave in a trail of disruption and death. I have the power to shake tall trees until their leaves fall down, covered in water, and scatter exiles far from their lands. I carry the bodies and souls of human beings on my back. Where do I retreat to, and what is my name?

**67**. My garment is darkish. Bright decorations, red and radiant, I have on my raiment. I mislead the stupid and stimulate the foolish toward unwise ways. Others I restrain from profitable paths. But I know not at all that they, maddened, robbed of their senses, astray in their actions—that they praise to all men my wicked ways. Woe to them then when the Most High holds out his dearest of gifts if they do not desist first from their folly.

**68**. I am a lonely thing, wounded with iron, smitten by sword, sated with battle-work, weary of blades. Often, I see battle, fierce combat. I foresee no comfort, no help will come for me from the heat of battle until among men I perish utterly; the hammered swords will beat me and bite me, hard-edged and sharp, the handiwork of smiths, in towns among men. Abide I must always the meeting of foes. Never could I find among the leeches, where people foregather, any who with herbs would heal my wounds; but the sores from the swords are always greater with mortal blows day and night.

**69**. I war oft against wave and fight against wind, do battle with both, when I reach to the ground, covered by the waters. The land is strange to me. I am strong in the strife if I stay at rest. If I fail at that, they are stronger than I and forthwith they wrench me and put me to rout. They would carry away what I ought to defend. I withstand them then if my tail endures and the stones hold me fast. Ask what my name is.

**70**. Beautifully made in many ways is this our world, cunningly adorned. Marvelous is its motion, I saw this device grind against the gravel, crying out as it went. This marvelous thing had no sight nor feeling, neither shoulders nor arms. One foot only had this curious device to journey along on, to move over the fields. It had many ribs, its mouth was midway. Useful to mortals, it bears abundance of food to the people, brings them plenty and pays to men annual tribute which all enjoy, the high and the lowly. Explain if you can, who are wise in words, what this thing may be.

**71.** What is the sister of the sun, though made for the night? The fire causes her tears to fall, and when she is near dying, they cut off her head. (by Jewish scholar Moses ibn Ezra, ca. 1070–1138)

**72.** What speaks in all languages in his riding, and his mouth spits the poison of life or death? It is silent when it rests, and it is deaf like a boy or one of the poor. (by tenth-century Jewish poet Dunash ben Labrat)

**73.** Truly no one is outstanding without me, nor fortunate; I embrace all those whose hearts ask for me. He who goes without me goes about in the company of death; and he who bears me will remain lucky forever. But I stand lower than earth and higher than heaven. (by Tatwine, archbishop of Canterbury, eighth century)

**74.** An eater lacking mouth and even maw; yet trees and beasts to it are daily bread. Well fed it thrives and shows a lively life, but give it water and you do it dead. (from *One Thousand and One Nights*, based on an older riddle; the earliest mention of the work is in the tenth century CE)

**75.** What is it that's blind with an eye in its head, but the race of mankind its use cannot spare; spends all its life in clothing the dead, but always itself is naked and bare? (by twelfth-century Jewish poet Jehudah Halevi)

**76.** I'm soft as wool, soft as a bog. When I swell up, I'm like a frog. I grow in water, where I plunge. (from *The History of Apollonius of Tyre*, ninth century)

**77.** I carry a greater load dead than alive. While I lie, serving many men; if I were to stand, I should serve a few. If my entrails are torn out to lie open out of doors, I bring life to all, and I give sustenance to many. A lifeless creature which bites nothing, when loaded down I run on my way yet never show my feet. (from *The Berne Riddles*, most likely composed by the seventh-century Irish monk Tullius)

**78.** Tell me, what is that fills the sky and the whole earth and tears up new shoots, and shakes all foundations, but cannot be seen by eyes or touched by hands? (by the Venerable Bede, 673-735 CE)

Incipit epistola sancti iheronimi ad
paulinum presbiterum de omnibus
diuine historie libris capitulu primu.

FRater ambrosius
tua michi munus-
cula perferens detulit
simul et suauissimas
literas q̃ a principio
amicicias fide pba-
te iam fidei et veteris amicicie noua:
pferebant. Vera enim illa necessitudo ē-
et xpi glutino copulata: quam non vtili-
tas rei familiaris: non pñtia tantum
corporu: nõ subdola et palpãs adulaco:
sed dei timor: et diuinaru scripturaru
studia conciliant. Legimus in veteribz
historijs: quosdã lustrasse puincias:
nouos adiisse pplos: maria transisse:
ut eos quos ex libris nouerant: corã
qq̃ viderent. Sicut pitagoras memphi-
ticos vates: sic plato egiptu et architã
tarentinu: eandemq̃ oram ytalie: que
quondã magna grecia dicebat̃: labo-
riosissime peragrauit: et ut qui athenis
magř erat et potens: cuiusq̃ doctrinas
achademie gignasia psonabãt: fieret
peregrinus atq̃ discipulus: malens aliena
verecunde discere: quam sua impudenter ingerere.
Deniq̃ cu literas quasi toto orbe fugien-
tes psequit̃ capt̃ a piratis et venunda-
tus: tyranno crudelissimo paruit: ductus
captiuus vinct̃ et seruus. Tamen quia
philosophus maior emente se fuit: ad tytum
liuium lacteo eloquencie fonte manante
de ultimis hispanie galliarumq̃ finibz
quosdam venisse nobiles legimus: et
quos ad contemplacionē sui roma nõ
traxerat: unius hois fama pduxit. Ha-
buit illa etas inauditu omnibz seculis:
celebranduq̃ miraculu: ut urbē tantã

ingressi: aliud extra urbem quererent.
Appollonius siue ille magus ut vulgus
loquitur: siue philosophus ut pitagorici tra-
dunt: intrauit psas: pteriuit caucasũ:
albanos: scithas: massagetas: opulen-
tissima indie regna penetrauit: et ad
extremu latissimo physon amne
tãsmisso: peruenit ad bragmanas: ut
hyarcam in throno sedente aureo et de
tantali fonte potantem: inter paucos
discipulos: de natura: de moribz: ac de
cursu dieru: et sideru: audiret docentem.
Inde p elamitas: babilonios: chalde-
os: medos: assyrios: parthos: syros:
phenices: arabes: palestinos: reuersus
ad alexandriã: perrexit ad ethiopiã:
ut gignosophistas et famosissimam
solis mensam videret in sabulo. Inue-
nit ille vir ubiq̃ q̃ disceret: et semp
proficiens: semp se melior fieret. Scrip-
sit super hoc plenissime octo volumi-
nibus: phylostratus.

Quid loquar de secli hominibz:
cum apostolus paulus: vas electionis:
et magister gentiũ: qui de consciencia
tãti in se hospitis loquebat̃ dicens. An
experimentum queritis eius qui in me
loquit̃ xps. Post damascũ arabiãq̃
lustratã: ascendit iherosolimã ut videret
petru et mãsit apud eũ diebz quindeci.
Hoc enim misterio ebdomadis et ogdo-
adis: futur̃ gentiũ pdicator instruen-
dus erat. Rursuq̃ post ãnos quatuor-
decim assumpto barnaba et tyto: expo-
suit cũ aplis euãgeliũ: ne forte in va-
cuum curreret aut cucurrisset. Habet
nescio q̃d latentis energie: viue vocis
actus: et in aures discipuli de auctoris
ore transfusa: forcius sonant. Unde et
eschineus cũ rodi exularet: et legeretur

## CHAPTER 3

# THE SPREAD OF LITERACY: RIDDLES IN THE RENAISSANCE

*"To learn to read is to light a fire; every syllable that is spelled out is a spark."* —VICTOR HUGO (1802–1885)

A paradigm-shifting event occurred around the middle part of the 1400s—the development of movable type technology, an event that made it possible to print and duplicate books and other written materials cheaply and massively. The Canadian communications theorist Marshall McLuhan (1911–1980) named the type of world order that ensued from that technological event the "Gutenberg Galaxy," after Johannes Gutenberg (ca. 1400–1468), the German printer who invented the printing press in Europe.[21]

A PAGE FROM THE GUTENBERG BIBLE, CA. 1455.

The Gutenberg Galaxy, as McLuhan observed, established printed books as the primary tools for recording and preserving information and knowledge, ushering in the Renaissance and the beginning of secular culture in place of scholastic theological culture. The Renaissance engendered the worldview known as *humanism*, an outlook that attached primary importance to human rather than divine matters. Literacy became a social value in the period—for everyone, not just those in authority. This led to an ever-broadening print-based culture, with books gaining enormous value and significance.

Riddle collections had achieved significant literary, educational, recreational, and religious value in the medieval period. However, literacy rates were still low, remaining largely the privilege of the few. Until the 1400s, paper documents were written by hand. Copyists, called "scribes," many of whom were monks, made duplicates of documents and books in monasteries. The riddle books discussed in the previous chapter were all produced in this way. By the fifteenth century, however, an easier and more efficient way to reproduce documents emerged. In 1450, Gutenberg perfected movable metal type technology, introducing the mechanical printing press for reproducing numerous copies of paper documents. The number of printing shops grew dramatically over the subsequent century, publishing not only books, but also newspapers, pamphlets, and other kinds of print materials.

As a result of the printing press, more and more people aspired to become literate, because with literacy came exposure to new ideas and independent thinking. With independent thinking came revolutions of religious, political, social, and scientific natures. Moreover, since cheaply printed books could be sent all over the world, scientists, philosophers, artists, educators, historians, poets, and storywriters read and translated one another's works. Ideas started crossing borders and vast spaces, uniting the world more, and standardized procedures in the scientific and business domains emerged. The invention of the printing press in the Renaissance paved the way to a world civilization.

Collections of riddles were among the first books printed, indicating that reading for pleasure was one of the first offshoots of the spread of literacy. A book of riddles called *Demaundes Joyous* (*Amusing Questions*) was published in England in 1511 by a printer named Wynkyn de Worde (a rather appropriate eponym). His book includes the famous paradoxical conundrum "Which came first, the chicken or the egg?" However, this book was not intended to educate children, but to provide humor and intellectual challenge to an adult audience, indicating that literacy was spreading into all domains and class levels of society. Here is a riddle from *Demaundes Joyous*:

79. WHICHE IS THE BRODEST WATER AND LEEST JEOPERDYE TO PASS OUER TRANSLATION: WHICH IS THE BROADEST WATER THAT POSES THE LEAST JEOPARDY TO PASS OVER?

## A Curious Thing

Starting in the 500s and up until the advent of the printing press, monks reproduced manuscripts by hand in scriptoriums, writing rooms in monasteries. The term "manuscript" means "written by hand," indicating that medieval books were handwritten. The printing press revolutionized European bookmaking, leading the way to worldwide mass communication that evolved into one based on electronic media in the twentieth century, and certainly the present one, rather than print.

AN 1891 ILLUSTRATION OF A SCRIBE.

WYNKYN DE WORDE'S PRINTING MARK, CA. 1500.

De Worde was born in Germany, but his date of birth is unknown. He emigrated to London around 1476 to work for William Caxton, the first person in England to run a printing press. After Caxton's death, De Worde took over the business, producing over four hundred books that ranged from religious treatises and children's books to romantic novels. He was the first printer to use italic font and Hebrew and Arabic characters, along with using movable typesetting to print music. His *Demaundes Joyous* is considered the oldest English book of jokes because the answers to the riddles are somewhat humorous. Below is an example (written in modern English):

### 80. HOW MANY CALVES' TAILS WOULD IT TAKE TO REACH FROM THE EARTH TO THE SKY?

Shortly after de Worde's collection was published, another popular riddle book appeared in 1575 titled *The Merry Book of Riddles*. This book was followed by a book with a very similar title, *The Booke of Merrie Riddles* in 1617. The latter likely had an educational function, as its subtitle, *Very Meet and Delightful for Youth to Try Their Wits*, implies. Here is an example from *The Booke of Merrie Riddle*s:

### 81. I WOUND THE HEART AND PLEASE THE EYE. TELL ME WHAT I AM, BY AND BY.

As literacy spread, the riddle genre attracted intellectuals, scientists, and philosophers of the era. Among them was Leonardo da Vinci (1452–1519), who wrote a set of "prophecies" as riddles, in which he portrayed hypothetical scenarios that the reader was challenged to figure out (typically providing answers to each one). The prophecies were written on sheets in the *Codex Atlanticus*, a collection of Da Vinci's writings and drawings compiled after his death by the Milanese sculptor Pompeo Leoni and now preserved in the Biblioteca Ambrosiana in Milan. The *Codex* is made up of 1,119 large sheets, which feature writing and illustrations on both sides. Da Vinci left them in his will to his trusted pupil, Giovan Francesco Melzi. Leoni procured Da Vinci's papers and notebooks from Melzi's heirs and assembled them into the *Codex Atlanticus*.

The prophecies seem, on the surface, to predict things to come, but the answers allude to everyday things and notions:

### 82. MEN WILL BE BORNE UP ON THE FEATHERS OF FLYING CREATURES.

**83. MANY WILL HAVE THEIR LITTLE ONES TAKEN FROM THEM AND SLAUGHTERED AND CRUELLY QUARTERED.**

**84. MANY WILL MAKE HOMES FOR THEMSELVES IN ENTRAILS AND LIVE IN THEIR OWN ENTRAILS.**

Da Vinci had a wry sense of humor, so he most likely designed these riddles to ridicule the practice of prophecy that was in vogue at the time, deriding it as anachronistic in an age of humanism (besides, any prediction can come true if it's vague enough). Among the most celebrated prophets of the era was Nostradamus (1503–1566), the Latinized name of the French astrologer and physician Michel de Nostredame, whose cryptic and apocalyptic prophecies were formulated as riddles, written in rhyming quatrains, in two collections—one in 1555 and one in 1558—and of which interpretation continues to be the subject of controversy.

The growth in popularity of riddle collections for seemingly trivial reasons was met by

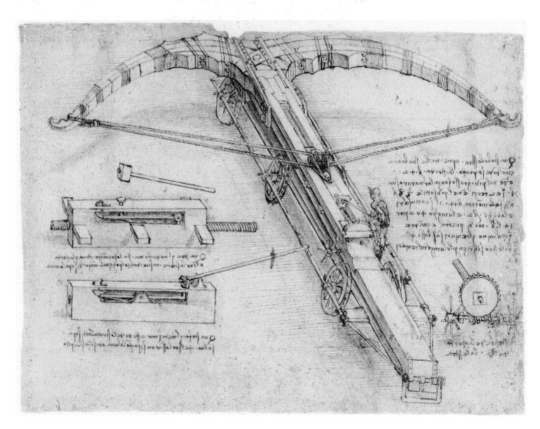

A PAGE FROM DA VINCI'S *CODEX ATLANTICUS*.

PORTRAIT OF BALDASSARE CASTIGLIONE BY RAPHAEL, CA. 1514–1515.

acerbic critiques. The Italian writer Baldassare Castiglione (1478–1529) attacked riddles in his 1528 book, *Il libro del cortegiano* (*The Book of the Courtier*), as instigations that promote insincerity among people and go against the ideals of virtue that the Renaissance espoused. But in the same era, virtue was dismissed as weakness, as can be seen in *The Prince* (1532) by Niccolò Machiavelli (1469–1527), where deceit, dissimulation, and mendacity are deemed "virtues" of power rather than damnable forms of behavior. The Renaissance was, clearly, an era of great contrasts.

From the 1400s to the late 1600s, the riddle evolved into a veritable literary art, shaped more and more by comedic and satirical style. As riddles increasingly became part of a literate recreational culture, the meaning of objects and their relation to human life became a major focus. But the ancient mythic or mystical element in riddling did not disappear; it became latent, as can be seen in the prophecies that were enunciated in riddle form.

To reiterate, after the advent of the printing press, riddle books were among the first to become popular throughout Europe as reading materials for leisure, providing both humor and poetic insight into the nature of things. Regarding the latter, the early 1500s German collection the *Strassburger rätselbuch* (*The Strasbourg Riddle Book*) is evidence of this, seeing as each riddle is a capsule of poetic insight:

**85. There came a bird featherless who sat on a tree. There came a maiden speechless and ate the bird featherless from off the tree leafless.**

The inclusion of riddles in larger narrative or dramatic works was another trend that emerged in the Renaissance. The great William Shakespeare (1564–1616) was a leader in this integrative use of the riddle. He used riddling as a kind of annotative commentary on the plot or theme in his plays. Here is an example from *Hamlet* (written between 1599 and 1602):

**86. What is he that builds stronger than either the mason, the shipwright, or the carpenter.**

One of the gravediggers poses this riddle to another before they run into Hamlet. It thematically fits in with the play's theme of the inevitability of death and the ineluctability of time. "A gravedigger," which is the answer, faces this reality more than anyone else (the mason, the shipwright, or the carpenter). What he builds (graves) is "strong," a metaphor for the power of death over everything.

The invention of the printing press had an enormous impact on everything from leisure to science. Well-known mathematicians, such as the Welshman Robert Recorde (ca. 1510–1558) and the Italians Niccolò Fontana Tartaglia (ca. 1499–1557) and Girolamo Cardano

## A Curious Thing

### THROUGHOUT HISTORY, RIDDLES HAVE HAD VARIOUS FUNCTIONS:

**MYSTICAL.** Many of the ancient riddles, such as those connected to the Oedipus legend and to Homer, had a mystical or prophetic function. This continued in the Renaissance with the use of prophecies of diviners in the era.

**RECREATIONAL.** Riddle contests have always been part of recreational culture. Their use at feasts, including the Roman Saturnalia and the Greek symposium, exemplified this function.

**EDUCATIONAL.** Many medieval riddle collections had an educational objective, including those of Aldhelm and Alcuin. This spread to the Renaissance, with the use of riddles for educating children—a function that has persisted to this day.

**HUMOR.** Many of the first printed riddle books were designed to evoke humor.

**LITERARY.** As riddles became more independent of mystical and educational traditions, they evolved into an autonomous literary genre.

*A GAME OF CHARADES* BY EDWARD MATTHEW WARD, CA. 1840.

(1501–1576), increasingly employed the puzzle format to illustrate and debate mathematical concepts. Like Alcuin, they saw riddles and puzzles as part of an expanding paradigm within which ideas could be formulated and tested. For example, the following puzzle, devised by Tartaglia, has all the characteristics of a riddle:

### 87. A MAN DIES, LEAVING SEVENTEEN CAMELS TO BE DIVIDED AMONG HIS HEIRS, IN THE PROPORTIONS ONE-HALF, ONE-THIRD, AND ONE-NINTH. HOW CAN THIS BE DONE?

Dividing up the camels in this manner would mean having to physically divide the camels, therefore killing them. So, Tartaglia suggested "borrowing an extra camel," for the sake of argument, not to mention humane reasons. Now with eighteen camels, he arrived at a practical solution: one heir was given one-half of eighteen camels (or nine camels), another one-third of eighteen (or six camels), and lastly, one-ninth of eighteen (or two camels). Nine camels plus six plus two more add up to the original seventeen. The extra camel could then be returned to its owner. Whether or not this is a real mathematical solution, it provides a kind of comic relief akin to that provided by many riddles.

The spread of riddle books in the 1500s made literacy—specifically reading for knowledge and recreational purposes—more attainable, thus assigning to riddles new cultural functions as literary texts in themselves. Literacy impels people to view knowledge as existing independently, unlike in oral cultures, where it is associated with a wise orator. Thus, it gets people to focus on knowledge as an abstraction rather than something that is tied to a specific person.

Before literacy became widespread, humans lived primarily in oral cultures, based on the spoken word. The human voice conveys emotion; orators and their messages were perceived as inseparable. On the other hand, in book-based cultures, the written page, with its edges, margins, and sharply defined characters laid out in neatly layered rows or columns, prompts a linear-rational way of thinking. And because the writer is seldom present during the reading, the readers are free to interpret it as they please. It is the "object" that comes out of the reading process—the meaning extracted from the reading itself. Within this mind-set, riddling became an abstract literary art, breaking away from myth or folklore.

# SOLVE THESE RENAISSANCE RIDDLES

(THE ANSWERS START ON PAGE 129)

RIDDLES 88 TO 94 ARE FROM *DEMAUNDES JOYOUS* BY WYNKYN DE WORDE. DO NOT LOOK FOR SOMETHING ABSTRACT OR RECHERCHÉ, JUST THE "OBVIOUS."

**88.** What thing is it that hath no end?
(HINT: IT IS A RECEPTACLE WHOSE SHAPE IMPLIES "NO END.")

**89.** What is the distance from the surface of the sea to the deepest part thereof?
(HINT: IN HUMOROUS STYLE, DE WORDE IS ALLUDING TO AN IDIOMATIC EXPRESSION.)

**90.** How may a man discern a cow in a flock of sheep?
(HINT: THE WORD "DISCERN" IS KEY TO SOLVING THIS RIDDLE.)

**91.** Why does a cow lie down?
(HINT: THINK OF SOMETHING OBVIOUS WITH REGARDS TO A COW.)

THE SAME TYPE OF HINT AS FOR RIDDLE 91—THINK OF THE OBVIOUS— APPLIES TO RIDDLES 91 TO 93.

**92.** What is it that never freezes?

**93.** How many straws go to a goose's nest?

**94.** How would you say two paternosters (Lord's Prayer), when you know God made but one paternoster?

**95.** A riddle from *The Booke of Merrie Riddles*: When I did live, then was I dumb, and yield no harmony: But being dead, I do afford most pleasant melody.

RIDDLES 96 TO 100 ARE FROM DA VINCI'S *CODEX ATLANTICUS*. RECALL THAT THESE ARE FRAMED AS PROPHETIC SCENARIOS.

**96.** Men will take pleasure in seeing their own work worn out and destroyed.

**97.** That shall come forth from hollow caves which shall cause all the nations of the world to toil and sweat with great agitation, anxiety, and labor, in order to gain its aid.

**98.** Many there will be who with the utmost zeal and solicitude will pursue furiously that which has always filled them with awe, not knowing its evil nature.

**99.** Men shall walk without moving, they shall speak with those who are absent, they shall hear those who do not speak.

**100.** Men shall come forth out of the graves changed to winged creatures, and they shall attack other men, taking away their food even from their hands and tables.

RIDDLES 101 TO 103 ARE FROM SHAKESPEARE'S *MERCHANT OF VENICE*. EACH OF THE RIDDLES IS INSCRIBED INSIDE A CASKET, AND IN THE FOLLOWING VERSIONS OF THE RIDDLES, YOU ARE ASKED TO INFER WHAT EACH CASKET IS MADE OF.

**101**. Who chooseth me shall gain what many men desire.

**102**. Who so chooseth me shall get as much as he deserves.

**103**. Who chooseth me must give and hazard all he hath.

THE REMAINING RIDDLES ARE FROM THE SIXTEENTH AND SEVENTEENTH CENTURIES, WITH UNKNOWN OR SKETCHY SOURCES.

**104**. He went to the wood and caught it. He sate him downe and sought it. Because he could not finde it, home with him he brought it.

**105**. Four wings I have, which swiftly mount on high, on sturdy pinions, yet I never fly. And though my body often moves around, upon the self-same spot I'm always found. And, like a mother, who breaks her infant's bread, I chew for man before he can be fed.

**106**. I am a merry creature in pleasant time of year. As in but certain seasons, I sing that you can hear. And yet I'm made of wood. A very perfect mock. Compared to foolish persons. And silliest of all folk.

**107**. I am the solution to finding what it is you're looking for. People do this every day to find out more.

AN ETCHING OF SHYLOCK FROM *THE MERCHANT OF VENICE*, BY JOHN HAMILTON MORTIMER, MARCH 15, 1776.

VOL. XLVIII. No. 1232.

PUCK BUILDING, New York, October 17th, 1900.
Copyright, 1900, by Keppler & Schwarzmann.

PRICE TEN CENTS.

"What fools these Mortals be!"

# Puck

Entered at N. Y. P. O. as Second-class Mail Matter.

THE RIDDLE OF THE SPHINX.

# CHAPTER 4

# CHARADES, ENIGMAS, AND CONUNDRUMS: RIDDLES AS PART OF LEISURE CULTURE

*"I like to be entertained, not smothered with 'literary' riddles."* —DAN JENKINS (1928–2019)

As literacy continued to spread after the Renaissance, riddles became part of an ever-broadening leisure culture. With the Industrial Revolution and the trend toward urbanization in the eighteenth and nineteenth centuries, this type of culture spread throughout society, as people acquired the economic possibility to engage in recreation, hobbies, and various pastimes. In other words, the Industrial Revolution gave common people the financial means to seek pleasure on its own. From the outset, this democratization of culture was viewed by some critics as encouraging

A POLITICAL CARTOON FROM *PUCK* MAGAZINE FEATURING WILLIAM JENNINGS BRYAN APPEALING TO A SPHINX WITH THE FACE OF FORMER PRESIDENT GROVER CLEVELAND, OCTOBER 17, 1900.

the rise and spread of a vulgar and degrading form of culture.

The British social critic and writer Matthew Arnold (1822–1888) saw it as a "dumbed down" version of true culture. Arnold believed that the kind of mass society that coalesced in the Industrial Age, when so-called "profane" culture became prominent, stunted human growth and potential.

However, forms of popular, or profane, culture have always existed, from ancient feasts, such as the Saturnalia, to medieval carnivals. The Industrial Revolution simply enabled the spread of this type of culture to anyone—it didn't increase or decrease its prevalence. In contrast to what critics like Arnold believed, there was actually the growth of a "literary culture" in his era, in which all kinds of reading materials became popular throughout society. Riddles were included among those materials as regular features in newspapers and periodicals, and writers took to riddling en masse. The French satirist Voltaire would regularly compose mind-teasing riddles such as this one:

**108. What of all things in the world is the longest, the shortest, the swiftest, the slowest, the most divisible and most extended, most regretted, most neglected, without which nothing can be done, and with which many do nothing, which destroys all that is little and ennobles all that is great?**

The answer is "time," which is often described metaphorically as "long," "short," "swift," "slow," "divisible," "extended," etc. Voltaire's riddle impels us to think about how we conceptualize time.

Given its spread throughout society, riddling spawned several derivative types. Three of these —the charade, the enigma, and the conundrum— developed into literary trends in the early part of the eighteenth century. The charade is a riddle solved by unraveling the various meanings

JANE AUSTEN FROM AN ORIGINAL FAMILY PORTRAIT.

suggested by the separate syllables, words, or lines in its statement. Here's a typical example: [22]

**109. My first is to ramble; My next to retreat; My whole oft enrages in summer's fierce heat. Who Am I?**

The answer is "gadfly." The phrase "My first" refers to the first syllable in "gadfly," namely "gad," which means "to move about by rambling"; the phrase "My next" refers to the second syllable in "gadfly," namely "fly," which means "to flee or retreat from something" or "a dipterous insect." The remainder of the riddle completes the description of the gadfly as an irritating insect.

Although charades were published as early as the 1740s in England, the term itself did not come into use until the late 1770s, differentiating it from the more common terms of "riddle" or "enigma." It likely was adapted from the Provençal *charrado*, meaning "conversation." Charades became a literary trend in themselves, adopted by such famous writers as Jane Austen (1775–1817). She included the following one in her 1816 novel, *Emma*:

**110. When my first is a task to a young girl of spirit, And my second confines her to finish the piece. How hard is her fate! but how great is her merit, If by taking my whole she effects her release!**

The charade has antecedents, as we saw with several medieval riddles. But it was never recognized as a genre of riddling until the eighteenth century, when it started being published in magazines, books, and even on handheld fans (the answers were on the reverse side of the fan, suggesting that they may have been courtship strategies that women used to entice suitors or tease paramours). People from all walks of life, not just writers, became adept at creating charades. And the charade eventually made its way to America, where it also became a fad of sorts. Here's a charade thought to have been one of President Theodore Roosevelt's favorites:

**111. I talk, but I do not speak my mind. I hear words, but I do not listen to thoughts. When I wake, all see me. When I sleep, all hear me. Many heads are on my shoulders. Many hands are at my feet. The strongest steel cannot break my visage. But the softest whisper can destroy me. The quietest whimper can be heard.**

Some of the earliest charades in America were published in the *Penny Post*, a magazine founded in Philadelphia in 1769. The term "charade" was not used in this publication, however. The first recorded use of the term was in the February 1789 issue of *The Massachusetts Magazine*. Charades started appearing thereafter in several magazines—all of which were intended

*The Solution of a Riddle.*

THE FRONTISPIECE FROM A 1792 BOOK TITLED *A CHOICE COLLECTION OF RIDDLES, CHARADES, REBUSSES, ETC.* BY PETER PUZZLEWELL.

for the upwardly mobile readers of the middle class. This example is from the March 1790 issue of *The New-York Magazine*:

**112.** MY FIRST THE EAR DOTH OFT DELIGHT, WITH MUSIC SWEET BOTH MORN AND NIGHT: MY NEXT IS VERY USEFUL FOUND, AS GOOD MANURE FOR THE GROUND: UNTO MY FIRST, MY WHOLE IS A SNARE, WHICH YOUTHFUL HANDS OFT PLACE WITH CARE.

For the answer, "birdlime" (an adhesive substance for trapping birds), the first part refers to the "music sweet" that is associated with the song of a "bird," and the next one plays on the meaning of "lime" as "manure for the ground." The rest of the riddle defines "birdlime" as a "snare."

Although charades of this kind were part of the literary culture, the American Puritans' opinions about riddling—and anything that gained public response outside of religious sobriety, for that matter—were divided: some loved them as part of a growing leisure secular culture, and others condemned them as foolish. Whatever the case, the charade thrived in America, as it did in Europe.

By the first years of the nineteenth century, charades had evolved into a parlor game people played at parties or celebrations. Known as the mime, or acted, charade, the game involved teams acting out the relevant syllables in a word in pantomime. The game started in France and eventually spread to England, where it found its way into the plots of famous novels, such as Charlotte Brontë's *Jane Eyre* (1847) and William Makepeace Thackeray's *Vanity Fair* (1848). In the latter novel, the social success of the protagonist, Rebecca (Becky) Sharp, is guaranteed by her adeptness at playing the mime charade before Prince Regent.

Today, the mime charade is a common party activity, with its own set of rules and signals, including:

- The number of fingers at the beginning of a round indicates the number of syllables in the answer.
- Tugging an earlobe signifies "sounds like."
- Holding fingers or hands close together usually means a short word, such as "the" or "that."
- Moving fingers even closer together indicates "shorter."
- Moving them apart means "longer" or "more."
- The "come here" hand gesture is used to indicate that the team is close to getting the correct answer, thus encouraging them to keep guessing.
- The pronoun "I" is relayed by pointing to one's eye or chest.
- Nodding indicates "correct guess."

There are other conventional signals for referring to persons, titles, shows, quotations, verb tenses, and so on. For example, if the answer to the charade is "football," the syllables "foot" and "ball" are acted out by pointing to a foot and then cupping one's hands in a rounded fashion or else using a throwing gesture. In the twentieth century, the mime charade appeared on television game shows from *Stump the Stars* and *Celebrity Charades* on American television to *Give Us a Clue* on British TV and *Celebrity Game* on Australian TV.

The "enigma" is the second derivative of riddling. Although enigma originally referred to any riddle or puzzle, in the era of the charade, this term was constrained to mean a riddle in verse form with one or more veiled references to the answer in the statement itself. The following enigma was written by the British statesman George Canning (1770–1827):

**113. A word there is of plural number. Foe to ease and tranquil slumber; Any other word you take And add an "s" will plural make, But if you add an "s" to this, So strange the metamorphosis; Plural is plural now no more, And sweet what bitter was before.**

The English politician and man of letters Horace Walpole (1717–1797) came up with the following ingenious enigma, which is based on how we use specific adverbs to relate the days of the week to each other in temporal terms:

**114. Before my birth I had a name. But soon as born I chang'd the same; And when I'm laid within the tomb, I shall my father's name assume. I change my name three days together, Yet live but one in any weather.**

Before its "birth," the answer, "today," does indeed have a different name—"tomorrow." For example, if "today" is Monday, then from the perspective of the day before, Sunday, it is labeled "tomorrow." And when it is "laid within

IN *VANITY FAIR*, BECKY SHARP ASSUMES THE CHARACTER OF CLYTEMNESTRA, THE WIFE OF AGAMEMNON, IN A MIME CHARADE.

# A Curious Thing

HERE ARE COMMON RULES FOR PLAYING THE MIME CHARADE:

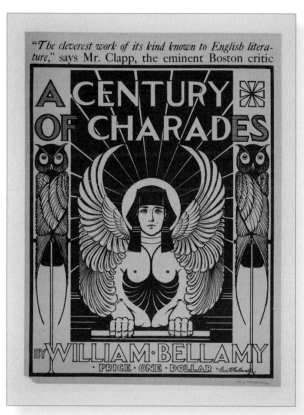

"The cleverest work of its kind known to English literature," says Mr. Clapp, the eminent Boston critic

A CENTURY OF CHARADES

BY WILLIAM·BELLAMY
·PRICE·ONE·DOLLAR·

A POSTER FOR WILLIAM BELLAMY'S BOOK *A CENTURY OF CHARADES*, WHICH IS ILLUSTRATED WITH A SPHINX, CA. 1900.

1. Players are divided into two or more teams.

2. One member on each team is secretly given the word on a piece of paper.

3. The person on each team who knows the word acts out the syllables in pantomime. Mouthing or pointing to objects are not allowed.

4. A timer is used to limit the guesses.

5. The number of correct guesses for each team, within the allotted time, are tallied on a scorecard.

6. Alternating team players is required until every player has acted at least once.

7. The number of correct guesses is established in advance as the winning tally.

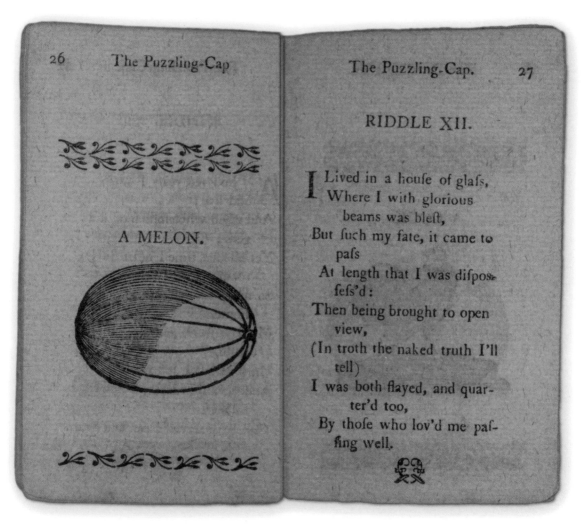

RIDDLE XII.

I Lived in a houſe of glaſs,
  Where I with glorious
    beams was bleſt,
But ſuch my fate, it came to
  paſs
  At length that I was diſpoſ-
  feſs'd :
Then being brought to open
  view,
(In troth the naked truth I'll
  tell)
I was both flayed, and quar-
  ter'd too,
  By thoſe who lov'd me paſ-
  ſing well.

A MELON.

**WITH ENIGMAS REFERRING TO COMMON OBJECTS, *THE PUZZLING-CAP* WAS PRINTED BY JOHN ADAMS IN 1805.**

the tomb," that is, when it is over, it takes a new name, "yesterday"—when Tuesday comes about, Monday is over, and we refer to it as "yesterday." Finally, though it lasts only one day, it changes its name three days in a row ("three days together") from "yesterday" to "today" to "tomorrow."

Some of the ancient and medieval riddles, including those by Symphosius and Aldhelm, were enigmas. The English author Jonathan Swift (1667–1745) was among the first to compose enigmas for pure pleasure. Below is his enigma about vowels from *Humorous Poems* (compiled by Bliss Carman et al. in the 1904 collection titled *The World's Best Poetry*):

**115. We are little airy creatures, all of different voice and features. One of us in glass is set, One of us you'll find in jet. T'other you may see in tin, and the fourth a box within. If the fifth you should pursue, it can never fly from you.**

The answer is "A, E, I, O, U": the vowel A is in "glass," E in "jet," I in "tin," O in "box," and U in "pursue" and "you."

Enigmas became popular in America with the 1787 publication of *The Little Puzzling Cap* in Worcester, Massachusetts. Most of the book's enigmas referred to common material objects known to the people of the era, including pots, melons, spectacles, oysters, and the like. Here is an enigma from the collection (the rhyme and focus are on the parts of the object being alluded to, which is typical of all enigmas):

**116. Can you the name of me devise? My mouth is formed like a bow, A nose I have, and many eyes, From whence my tears do often flow; I seldom weep in winter time, Although the weather is ne'er so cold; But when gay Floral's in her prime, My tears you often may behold.**

There is no known copy of this book in existence today, which is somewhat strange given that various editions were released under different titles in several New England cities. In fact, editions were also published in the early 1800s in New York, Philadelphia, and Hartford.

Alongside charades and enigmas, the same era saw the rise and spread of the conundrum, a riddle that plays on the similar sounds of word pairs, such as "red" and "read" (homophony), and the different meanings of words or expressions, such as "all over" (double entendre).[23] Here's an example:

**117. What is black and white and red all over?**

This particular riddle with the answer of a "newspaper" has appeared in many American publications since 1917, constituting what some riddle scholars call a "folk riddle," which is a riddle that becomes part of an unconscious folk culture. This type is sometimes called a "neck riddle," going back to the Exeter Book and alluding to the fact that some folk heroes can "save their neck" by outwitting a nefarious riddler. A conundrum is essentially a riddle joke, and in fact, the conundrum above can lead to different humorous answers, such as "a penguin with a rash." As linguist Delia Chiaro observes, riddles of this kind are virtually impossible to translate into other languages, implying that, unlike many other kinds of riddles, they are based on the specific structures and forms of one language.[24] Incidentally, the origin of the word "conundrum" is generally traced to England in the late sixteenth century, as a pseudo-Latin word among scholars at Oxford University that referred to a "silly or picayune individual."

Conundrums can also be based on punning, the play on different possible meanings of a word (known as polysemy) or a play on words that sound alike but have different meanings. Here's an example of such a riddle:

### 118. WHAT CAN BE SWALLOWED OR CAN SWALLOW SOMEONE?

For the answer, "pride," the word "swallow" can refer to different things, as exemplified in the expressions "He had to swallow his pride" and "Pride can swallow you up." The determining factor is the context in which the word is used, bringing out its crucial role for deciphering the meaning of all riddles.

Many interesting conundrums are found in one of the earliest publications of puzzle materials in America, *An Almanack for the Year of Our Lord 1647*, printed in Cambridge, Massachusetts, by Samuel Danforth (1626–1674), who was a Puritan minister, poet, and astronomer. He was also well known during his time as a staunch defender of Scripture. Danforth published four almanacs, which are among the oldest ones preserved. Below is a conundrum, which may also pass as an enigma, from one of his almanacs:

### 119. GREAT BRIDGES SHALL BE MADE ALONE, WITHOUT AX, TIMBER, EARTH, OR STONE. OF CHRYSTALL METALL, LIKE TO GLASS; SUCH WONDROUS WORKS SOON COME TO PASSE, IF YOU MAY THEN HAVE SUCH A WAY. THE FERRY-MAN YOU NEED NOT PAY.

Samuel Cheever, of whom almost nothing is known, followed on Danforth's coattails with his *An Almanack for the Year of Our Lord 1660*. However, the best known of all the almanacs was *Poor Richard's Almanack* by Benjamin Franklin (1706–1790), which was first published in 1732 under the pen name Richard Saunders. In the 1736 edition, Franklin wrote three ingenious enigmas he referred to as "enigmatical prophecies," recalling Leonardo da Vinci's "prophecies." Here's one of them:

### 120. NOT LONG AFTER (THE MIDDLE OF THE YEAR) A VISIBLE ARMY OF 20000 MUSKETERS WILL LAND, SOME IN VIRGINIA & MARYLAND, AND SOME IN THE LOWER COUNTIES ON BOTH SIDES OF DELAWARE, WHO WILL OVER-RUN THE COUNTRY, AND SORELY ANNOY THE INHABITANTS: BUT THE AIR IN THIS CLIMATE WILL AGREE WITH THEM SO ILL TOWARD WINTER, THAT THEY WILL DIE IN THE BEGINNING OF COLD WEATHER LIKE ROTTEN SHEEP, AND BY CHRISTMAS THE INHABITANTS WILL GET THE BETTER OF THEM.

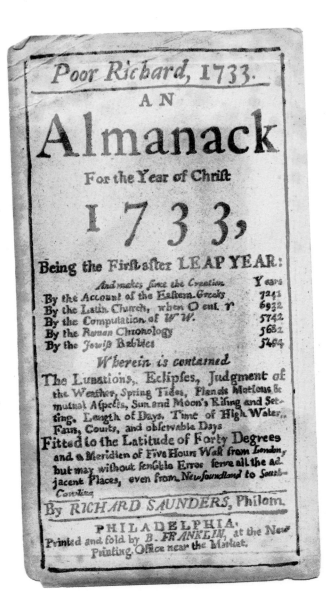

A FACSIMILE OF THE TITLE PAGE OF THE 1733 *POOR RICHARD'S ALMANACK.*

"The Army which it was said would land in Virginia, Maryland, and the Lower Counties on Delaware were not Musketers with Guns on their Shoulders as some expected; but their Namesakes, in Pronunciation, tho' truly spelt Moschitos, armed only with a sharp Sting . . . being bred in the Water; and therefore may properly be said to land before they become generally troublesome."

By the mid-eighteenth century, publications with enigmas, charades, and conundrums were proliferating. From this trend, the acrostic—a literary device in which the first letter of every verse consecutively forms a word or message—emerged. Literary acrostics are found throughout literature. Edgar Allan Poe composed the following acrostic poem, "Elizabeth" (in which the first letters of each line, when read from top to bottom, spell the name):

Elizabeth it is in vain you say
"Love not"—thou sayest it in so sweet a way:
In vain those words from thee or L. E. L.
Zantippe's talents had enforced so well:
Ah! if that language from thy heart arise,
Breath it less gently forth—and veil thine eyes.
Endymion, recollect, when Luna tried
To cure his love—was cured of all beside—
His folly—pride—and passion—for he died.

"L. E. L." was the signature of Letitia Elizabeth Landon, an English poet and novelist, whom Poe obviously admired. "Zantippe" is

Franklin withheld the answers to his enigmas until he put out his almanac of the subsequent year. In the 1737 edition, he explained the answer to this riddle, which is "mosquitoes":

A PORTRAIT OF LEWIS CARROLL (CHARLES LUTWIDGE DODGSON) IN 1855 AT THE AGE OF TWENTY-THREE.

**A** boat, beneath a sunny sky
**L**ingering onward dreamily
**I**n an evening of July—

**C**hildren three that nestle near,
**E**ager eye and willing ear,
**P**leased a simple tale to hear—

**L**ong has paled that sunny sky:
**E**choes fade and memories die:
**A**utumn frosts have slain July.

**S**till she haunts me, phantomwise.
**A**lice moving under skies
**N**ever seen by waking eyes.

**C**hildren yet, the tale to hear,
**E**ager eye and willing ear,
**L**ovingly shall nestle near.

**I**n a Wonderland they lie,
**D**reaming as the days go by,
**D**reaming as the summers die:

**E**ver drifting down the stream—
**L**ingering in the golden gleam—
**L**ife, what is it but a dream?

Poe's modified spelling of Xanthippe, the clever wife of Socrates (the original spelling wouldn't have worked in the acrostic).

Lewis Carroll also wrote scores of acrostic poems. The last poem in *Through the Looking-Glass* is an acrostic that hides the name "Alice Pleasance Liddell," who was likely the real-life inspiration for Carroll's famous character Alice:

Carroll's invention of the game of doublets is another example of how wordplay came to be considered a leisure activity in the Industrial Age. In this game, the solver is given two words—constituting the first and last steps—and they are required to "evolve" one word into

74

the other by changing only one letter at a time and forming a new word with each change. Here is Carroll's original puzzle:

**121. TURN THE WORD HEAD INTO TAIL, BY CHANGING ONLY ONE LETTER AT A TIME, FORMING A NEW WORD EACH TIME TO DO SO.**

The four words that are required are called "links." There are five links in the above doublet—namely, heal—teal—tell—tall—tail.

Carroll had, in fact, initially named the puzzle "word-links," which he mentioned in a diary entry of March 12, 1878. He soon changed his mind, calling it "doublet," which he derived from the witches' incantation in Shakespeare's *Macbeth*: "Double, double, toil and trouble." In his pamphlet *Word-links: A Game for Two Players, or a Round Game*, published in April 1878, Carroll says he created the game for two girls on Christmas Day of 1877, because they usually "found nothing to do." Given the popularity of the doublets he had published in *Vanity Fair*, the publisher Macmillan put out a thirty-nine-page booklet containing many of these puzzles in 1879, titled *Doublets: A Word Puzzle*. The name "doublet" has stuck ever since.

In his classic book, *Language on Vacation* (1965), Dmitri Borgmann (1927–1985) renamed the doublet "word ladder," which describes the solution strategy itself, consisting of "word steps" that are logically connected like the rungs of a ladder. For this reason, it is also called a "laddergram."

# SOLVE THESE CHARADES, EGNIMAS, AND CONUNDRUMS

(THE ANSWERS START ON PAGE 130)

RIDDLES 122 TO 129 ARE EXAMPLES OF LITERARY CHARADES. IN ALL THE PUZZLES, "MY FIRST" REFERS TO THE FIRST SYLLABLE OR WORD IN THE ANSWER, AND "MY SECOND" REFERS TO THE SECOND SYLLABLE OR WORD IN THE ANSWER.

**122**. My first makes me eligible for marriage as an equal, and my second makes me inferior. Overall, I am incomparable.

**123**. My first is someone who is always there, and my second is a large vessel. Together we form a close relationship.

**124**. My first is the foundation of things, my second a round object. Join us up and you will discover what Babe Ruth was famous for.

**125**. My first puts things higher than other things, and my second is where you might sit. Combine us and you get events or things that occur simultaneously.

**126**. My first is a delicate bird, and my second a hindmost part. Together we indicate how things can fit together.

**127**. My first is someone who exerts dominance, and my second is a portion. You should know that I am something outstanding.

**128**. My first is a spectacle; my second an instance. You should know that I exhibit things.

**129**. My first indicates pottery, and my second a habitation. I allow people to store things.

RIDDLES 130 AND 131 ARE CHARADES WRITTEN BY JANE AUSTEN. UNDERSTANDABLY, THEY ARE QUITE CHALLENGING.

**130**. My first doth affliction denote, which my second is destin'd to feel. And my whole is the best antidote that affliction to soften and heal.

**131**. My first displays the wealth and pomp of kings, Lords of the earth! Their luxury and ease. Another view of man, my second brings. Behold him there, the monarch of the seas! But ah! united, what reverse we have! Man's boasted power and freedom, all are flown; Lord of the earth and sea, he bends a slave. And woman, lovely woman, reigns alone. Thy ready wit the word will soon supply, May its approval beam in that soft eye!

**132.** What has four eyes but cannot see?

**133.** Change one letter in me and from an achievement I become a physical means of locomotion.

**134.** "I" am in a storm or in the wind, but I am spelled differently.

**135.** With a "T" at the end you can wear it; with an "M" instead, you can eat it.

**136.** Spelled one way I am colorful, spelled another way, but pronounced the same, I am something that is done to books.

**137.** On my face it makes me look foolish; in a famous riddle it constitutes a paradox about origins.

**138.** They protect you against the cold; but you have to take them off in a fight.

**139.** Smack them or curl them, they are the same body part.

**140.** If it's wild and you chase it, you will get nowhere.

**141.** You can see its colors, but don't chase it, because it too will get you nowhere.

**142.** Add an "R" and from a temperature I turn into a vital organ.

**143.** Breaking it relieves tension between people.

**144.** If you see its tip, then your real problem remains hidden.

**145.** Don't kick it, if you want to stay alive.

**146.** It is sweet and tasty; and a piece will make something easier.

**147.** I am delicious when hot, but also controversial.

**148.** Use them to sip something. However, the last one of these makes a situation unbearable.

**149.** Change one letter and from a wound I become a household companion.

Why is

A

Dog's
Tail

like

The heart of a tree?

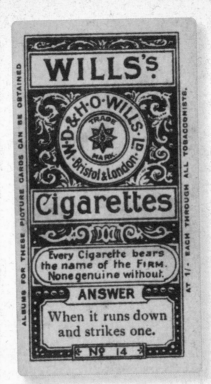

WILL'S.

W·D·& H·O·WILLS·Lᴰ

TRADE MARK

M·Bristol & London.

Cigarettes

Every Cigarette bears
the name of the FIRM.
None genuine without.

ALBUMS FOR THESE PICTURE CARDS CAN BE OBTAINED

AT 1/- EACH THROUGH ALL TOBACCONISTS.

ANSWER

When it runs down
and strikes one.

Nº 14

What is if which

A

Cat

has

but no other animal?

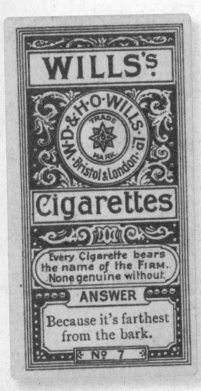

WILL'S.

W·D·& H·O·WILLS·Lᴰ

TRADE MARK

M·Bristol & London.

Cigarettes

Every Cigarette bears
the name of the FIRM.
None genuine without.

ANSWER

Because it's farthest
from the bark.

Nº 7

When is

A
Clock
on
the stairs dangerous?

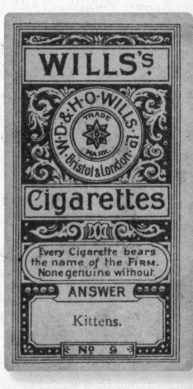

WILL'S.

W·D·& H·O·WILLS·Lᴰ

TRADE MARK

M·Bristol & London.

Cigarettes

Every Cigarette bears
the name of the FIRM.
None genuine without.

ANSWER

Kittens.

Nº 9

## CHAPTER 5

# INTO THE STORY: RIDDLES IN LITERATURE

*"Every great literature has always been allegorical—allegorical of some view of the whole universe. The 'Iliad' is only great because all life is a battle, the 'Odyssey' because all life is a journey, the Book of Job because all life is a riddle."*

—GILBERT K. CHESTERTON (1874–1936)

During the nineteenth century, an explosion of riddle and puzzle books were published. This is, arguably, anecdotal evidence that the middle class had benefited from increases in affluence, literacy rates, and leisure time. In the same era, riddles became associated with children's literature once and for all, recalling the riddles of the medieval era and the Renaissance, which were likely used to help children learn to read.

WILL'S BRAND CIGARETTE ADVERTISING CARDS WITH RIDDLES ON THEM, CA. LATE NINETEENTH TO EARLY TWENTIETH CENTURY.

In many of the children's stories of the nineteenth century, riddles exemplified human cleverness. For example, in the anonymous *The Hundred Riddles of the Fairy Bellaria* (1892), a queen named Bellaria with riddle-solving skills is pitted against a cruel, invading king named Ruggero. He gives her one hundred riddles to solve, and to fail would end in disaster. (Fun fact: the Riddler in Batman is a modern-day descendant of Ruggero.) Many tales composed for children in the same period were narrative riddles in themselves. Lewis Carroll's *Alice's Adventures in Wonderland* and *Through the Looking-Glass* are perfect examples of stories that not only contain riddles within them, but are also contrived as riddles in overall design.

Nursery rhymes of the era were often posed in riddle form. Here is a famous one that originated in eighteenth-century England:

**150. As I was going to St. Ives**
**I met a man with seven wives.**
**Each wife had seven sacks,**
**Each sack had seven cats,**
**Each cat had seven kits.**
**Kits, cats, sacks, wives,**
**How many were going to St. Ives?**

The riddle asks how many "kits," "cats," "sacks," and "wives" were "going to St. Ives," not "coming from" it. Only one person was "going to" St. Ives—the narrator of the rhyme. Two of the earliest versions of this riddle are in the August 4, 1779 issue of the *Weekly Magazine* and in a manuscript from around the year 1730. Interestingly, given the nuanced suggestion of polygamy ("a man with seven wives"), the earliest versions of this riddle eliminated the offensive part, and the version here became the standard one by the mid-nineteenth century.

Incidentally, this very riddle was used in the action movie *Die Hard with a Vengeance* (1995) as part of intellectual warfare mixed in with actual violence; it was used there as a riddle game, which hearkens back to the Riddle of the Sphinx—a contest of minds that appears in many famous writings ever since the Oedipus story. The "riddle game" became widespread in the Middle Ages as a street contest where entertainers would pose riddles, enticing visitors to pay them for the answers. In various traditional African cultures, riddle games were integral to coming-of-age rites in order to likely put the budding adult's mental prowess to the test.

Riddles played a key role in the collection *Children's and Household Tales* (1812) by the Brothers Grimm, which contains over two hundred traditional tales from medieval German culture. One such tale is even titled "The Riddle," which is about solving a riddle that will lead to a royal marriage. Much like the ancient Sphinx-type riddles, the tradition of the riddle game as proof of the solver's mettle is found throughout folk cultures.

The riddle game also made its way into contemporary literature. J. K. Rowling's popular *Harry Potter* novels (seven in total) contain the

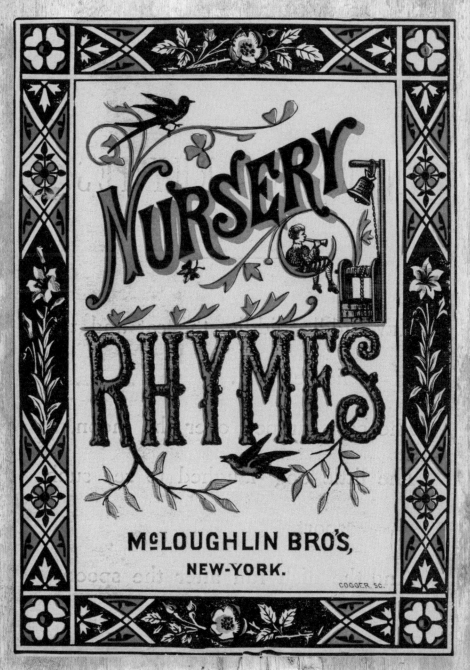

NURSERY RHYMES

McLOUGHLIN BRO'S,
NEW-YORK.

COGGER, SC.

A TITLE PAGE FROM A NINETEENTH-CENTURY COLLECTION OF NURSERY RHYMES.

The Hobbit JRR TOLKIEN

1998©

20

## A Curious Thing

As depicted by Tolkein, hobbits are small humanoid creatures inhabiting so-called Middle-earth. They appeared for the first time in *The Hobbit*. The name Gollum is evocative of the Golem, which in Jewish folklore is an anthropomorphic creature made of mud or clay that is animated through magic. *The Hobbit* was followed by *The Fellowship of the Ring* (1954), which was the first book in *The Lord of the Rings* trilogy. Much of the popularity of the Tolkein novels is likely due to their mythological structure and themes that evoke an ancient sapience to guide the modern world.

A 1998 POSTAGE STAMP FROM THE UNITED KINGDOM DEPICTING A SCENE FROM *THE HOBBIT*.

riddle game, which provides clues to reveal secrets. It is no coincidence that two characters in the series are named Thomas and Mary Riddle, who live in their so-called Riddle House. In J. R. R. Tolkein's *The Hobbit* (1937), Bilbo Baggins and the treacherous Gollum take part in a riddle game. If Bilbo wins the contest, Gollum must show him the way out of a tunnel in which he is lost; but if Bilbo loses, Gollum will devour him— again evoking the Riddle of Sphinx almost by direct citation. Here are two of Gollum's riddles:

**151. WHAT HAS ROOTS AS NOBODY SEES, IS TALLER THAN TREES, UP, UP IT GOES, AND YET NEVER GROWS?**

**152. VOICELESS IT CRIES, WINGLESS FLUTTERS, TOOTHLESS BITES, MOUTHLESS MUTTERS.**

AN ILLUSTRATION OF GOLLUM IN *THE HOBBIT*

The answer to the first riddle is "mountain," and the answer to the second one is "wind." The former describes features of mountains that may escape attention, depicting them in a metaphorical way and poetically connecting images. The latter depicts and blends the sensory experiences associated with the wind.

Bilbo wins the riddle contest by thinking out loud about what he has in his pocket, which Gollum thinks is a riddle: What have I got in my pocket? This is not really a riddle but a final challenge. Bilbo has the ring that Gollum is searching for in his pocket. The ring is a symbol of power and corruption, reaching back to similar symbolic uses of the ring in such works as Richard Wagner's four operas in the *Ring Cycle* (1874), which hearkens back to the medieval epic *Nibelungenlied*. Gollum lives a miserable, solitary life underground, away from the sun, with his beloved ring, while Bilbo, who isn't interested in power and wealth, wears the ring without being consumed by jealousy or vanity.

The riddle game scene takes place after Gollum goes to the place where he hides the ring and finds that it is missing. Gollum confronts Bilbo and asks him what is in his pocket. Bilbo, unaware of the ring's power, slips it on his finger as Gollum runs to attack him. Bilbo becomes invisible thanks to the ring's magical powers. Gollum then fears that without the ring, he will ultimately be captured by the race of Goblins. Bilbo decides against killing Gollum because it would be unfair, since Bilbo is invisible.

Even before *The Hobbit*, nineteenth-century authors were incorporating riddles into the storyline. Often, they were created to emphasize human foibles and the meaninglessness of human actions. They were common in a genre called "literary nonsense," which flourished in the Victorian era. The origin of the movement can be traced to the popularity of the nursery rhymes of Mother Goose—an imaginary author of French fairy tales, which became the basis for many English nursery rhymes. This pseudonym is traced to Charles Perrault's collection of fairy tales, *Contes de ma mere l'oye*, translated in English as *Tales of My Mother Goose* (1729). An example of a nonsense riddle from this collection is the following one:

Hey, diddle, diddle!
The cat and the fiddle,
The cow jumped over the moon;
The little dog laughed
To see such sport,
And the dish ran away with the spoon.

This riddle is designed to resist any specific meaning or interpretation. Literary scholars hypothesize that it has roots in medieval proverbs and literature. But there is little concrete evidence to support this. As in any nonsense work, searching for a meaning is itself nonsensical, inducing a kind of circular reasoning that never comes to a meaningful point.

It comes as little surprise that Lewis Carroll, one of the greatest puzzle makers of all time, became enmeshed in the trend of literary nonsense. Carroll's children's novels and poetry, especially *Alice's Adventures in Wonderland*, have a strong appeal in large part because of riddles that seem to lead nowhere, bringing out the inanity of life. His poems "Jabberwocky" (in *Through the Looking-Glass*) and "The Hunting of the Snark" (1876) are primary examples of the technique of literary nonsense. A famous nonsense riddle is the one posed by the Mad Hatter at his tea party in *Alice's Adventrues in Wonderland*:

"Why is a raven like a writing desk?"

* * *

"Have you guessed the riddle yet?"
The Hatter said, turning to Alice again.
"No. I give it up," Alice replied. "What's the answer?"
"I haven't the slightest idea," said the Hatter.
"Nor I," said the March Hare.
Alice sighed wearily. "I think you might

# HEY DIDDLE, DIDDLE.

Hey diddle diddle, the cat and the fiddle,
The Cow jumped over the moon,
The little dog laughed to see such sport,
And the dish ran away with the spoon

AN ILLUSTRATION FROM *OLD MOTHER GOOSE'S RHYMES & TALES* BY CONSTANCE HASLEWOOD, CA. 1890.

do something better with time than wasting it in asking riddles that have no answer."

"If you knew Time as well as I do," said the Hatter, "you wouldn't talk about wasting *it*. Time is not an it. It's *him*."

Readers were so frustrated by the lack of an answer in the novel that Carroll was compelled to provide an explanation in the preface of a later edition: "Enquiries have been so often addressed to me, as to whether any answer to the Hatter's Riddle can be imagined, that I may as well put on record here what seems to me to be a fairly appropriate answer, viz: 'Because it can produce a few notes, tho' they are very flat; and it is nevar put with the wrong end in front!' This, however, is merely an afterthought; the Riddle, as originally invented, had no answer at all."

In his answer, Carroll—ever the puzzlist—used the word "nevar," which seems at first to be a misspelling of "never." But it is the word "raven" spelled backward. In effect, there is no answer; the riddle is nonsense, no more no less. Nevertheless, it seems that people cannot leave an unsolved riddle alone. So, after publication of Carroll's purported explanation, the number of famous people who have attempted to answer it is very high. But there is no real answer—it is nonsense.

Even the names of some of the characters in *Alice* are part of Carroll's nonsense style. For example, the name of the character Dormouse

THE MAD HATTER'S TEA PARTY IN *ALICE'S ADVENTURES IN WONDERLAND*, ILLUSTRATED BY JOHN TENNIEL.

appears to have little real meaning: Is it a mouse that lives near a door? The character is a lazy person who is always sleepy, which reveals the source of his name as *dormeus* in Latin, which means "sleepy person." His poem about the killing of a strange creature called the Jabberwock in *Through the Looking-Glass* is one of Carroll's most salient examples of nonsense writing. Many of the words in the poem are unknown, but they appear to be legitimate English words, simply because they possess the normal grammatical and phonetic structure of English words. But they have no ascribed meaning. Carroll has, in effect, disconnected form from meaning, leaving it up to the imagination of the reader to figure out what the words could possibly mean:

'Twas brillig, and the slithy toves
Did gyre and gimble in the wabe:
All mimsy were the borogoves,
And the mome raths outgrabe.

"Beware the Jabberwock, my son!
The jaws that bite, the claws that catch!
Beware the Jubjub bird, and shun
The frumious Bandersnatch!"

He took his vorpal sword in hand:
Long time the manxome foe he sought
So rested he by the Tumtum tree,
And stood awhile in thought.

And, as in uffish thought he stood,
The Jabberwock, with eyes of flame,

Came whiffling through the tulgey wood,
And burbled as it came!

One, two! One, two! And through and through
The vorpal blade went snicker-snack!
He left it dead, and with its head
He went galumphing back.

"And hast thou slain the Jabberwock?
Come to my arms, my beamish boy!
O frabjous day! Callooh! Callay!"
He chortled in his joy.

'Twas brillig, and the slithy toves
Did gyre and gimble in the wabe:
All mimsy were the borogoves,
And the mome raths outgrabe.

We do get a sense of what happens in the poem by imagining what the words could mean. This style was adopted brilliantly by Dr. Seuss (Theodore Seuss Geisel, 1904–1991) in his children's books, which can be characterized as written in a Jabberwocky-style language.

English humorist Edward Lear (1812–1888) became famous for his nonsense writing. His books *A Book of Nonsense* (1846) and *Laughable Lyrics* (1877) are prototypical examples of this style, which continues in various forms today. Nonsense writing influenced various genres of twentieth-century literature, including the Theater of the Absurd, which is represented in the writings

## BEWARE THE JABBERWOCK

THE JABBERWOCK IN *THROUGH THE LOOKING-GLASS*. ILLUSTRATED
BY JOHN TENNIEL

of mental challenge on a regular basis—as the popularity of riddles across the world and across time attests.

Riddles in literature are now common. For example, Stephen King, famous for his horror and suspense stories and novels, used riddles as a central feature in his *Dark Tower* series of novels. The following riddle is from *Wizard and Glass* (*Dark Tower IV*, 1997):

**153. NOT CHEST OR BOX IS NOW DISCUSSED. MONEY CAN BE HELD IN IT, BUT JUST AS WE TEST ITS METAL, WITHIN IT THERE IS RUST.**

Another famous literary example goes back to the riddle that the character Stephen Dedalus posed to his pupil in James Joyce's (1882–1941) *Ulysses* (1922):

**154. THE COCK CREW, THE SKY WAS BLUE: THE BELLS IN HEAVEN WERE STRIKING ELEVEN. 'TIS TIME FOR THIS POOR SOUL TO GO TO HEAVEN.**

of playwrights like Samuel Beckett and Eugène Ionesco.

The French sociologist Émile Durkheim (1858–1917) saw myths as part of a "collective conscious," and thus common to every human being.[25] In the early myths, riddles were a primary means for grasping truths, as we saw with the Riddle of the Sphinx. For whatever reason, human beings seem to need this kind

The answer—"the fox burying his grandmother under a holly bush"—is not really an answer, but rather a play on the riddle form itself. It is a riddle about riddling, with Joyce, perhaps taking his cue from Lewis Carroll's Mad Hatter riddle.

Following in the tradition of the Victorian writers, the contemporary novelist Neil Gaiman (b. 1960) uses riddles in many of his works. The

following is an example of his riddling art from *The Books of Magic* (1990), which is a series of graphic novels:

### 155. WHEN THERE IS A FIRE INSIDE YOU, I AM STILL COLD.

Dan Brown (b. 1964), whose *Da Vinci Code* (2003) became one of the most lucrative bestsellers of all time, is yet another modern author who employs riddling as part of his narrative technique. The following riddle comes from his novel *Inferno* (2013), and the answer is the key to solving the main mystery in the novel:

### 156. THE TRUTH CAN BE GLIMPSED ONLY THROUGH THE EYES OF DEATH.

In Paris in 1960, a small group of writers and mathematicians who were devoted to exploring the relationship between wordplay and reality founded a society called Oulipo, short for Ouvroir de littérature potentielle (Workshop of Potential Literature). Oulipo defines "potential literature" as literature based on structures and patterns that writers may invent and use freely.

One of the Oulipo founders, Raymond Queneau (1903–1976), published a book of poetry titled *Cent mille milliards de poèmes* (*One Hundred Trillion Sonnets*, 1961) that has ten sonnets, one on each of ten pages. The pages of the book are cut into individual strips so that one can turn each of the fourteen lines of a sonnet separately. The book's physical format allows for one hundred trillion combinations of lines, which

2012

PLAC
G ORG S
P R C

CRIVAIN FRANÇAIS 1936 - 1982

A TRIBUTE TO GEORGES PEREC AT CAFÉ DE LA MAIRIE ON PLACE SAINT-SULPICE IN PARIS.

equal one hundred trillion sonnets. And Queneau claimed that all of them "make sense."

Georges Perec's (1936–1982) three-hundred-page novel, *La disparition* (*Disappearance*, 1969), is another example of an Oulipian work. No word in the novel contains the letter E, and yet it reads as fluidly as any other narrative. Such a work that omits a letter or letters is called a "lipogram." Perec insisted that his lipogrammatic novel was worthy of being considered literature, since it was designed to explore language's infinite possibilities.

American humorist James Thurber (1894–1961) also wrote a well-known lipogrammatic work in 1957, titled *The Wonderful O*. It's a political fable for children that tells the story of Captain Black, a literate pirate who hates the letter O, therefore banishing it from the island of Ooroo.

Another Oulipian technique is to make up sentences that contain all the letters of the alphabet, called "pangrams." Here are a few examples:[26]

Pack my box with five dozen liquor jugs.
    (32 letters)
A quick brown fox jumps over the lazy dog.
    (33 letters)
Waltz, nymph, for quick jugs vex Bud.
    (28 letters)
Quick wafting zephyrs vex bold Jim.
    (29 letters)

Lipograms and pangrams are proof that constraint on linguistic structure in no way limits the potential for meaning. The Oulipian approach shows us that we are inclined to extract meaning from words even when we artificially restrict the ways in which they can be made and used. The ancient riddlers sought to uncover hidden meanings in virtually the same way—by playing with meaning. Around 2,500 years ago, the Greek poet Pindar (ca. 522–443 BCE) foreshadowed the Oulipian method, writing an entire ode without using the letter sigma ($\Sigma$).[27]

# SOLVE THESE LITERARY AND CHILDREN'S RIDDLES

(THE ANSWERS START ON PAGE 133)

RIDDLES 157 TO 162 ARE FROM THE RIDDLE-GAME SCENE IN *THE HOBBIT*.

**157.** Thirty white horses on a red hill. First they champ [chomp]. Then they stamp. Then they stand still.

**158.** An eye in a blue face, saw an eye in a green face. "That eye is like to this eye," said the first eye, "but in low place, not in high place."
(HINT: THINK OF THE "EYE" AS PART OF AN ASTRAL BODY THAT SHINES ON FLOWERS OF DIFFERENT COLORS.)

**159.** It cannot be seen, cannot be felt, cannot be heard, cannot be smelt. It lies behind stars and under hills, and empty holes it fills. It comes first and follows after, ends life, kills laughter.

**160.** A box without hinges, key, or lid, yet golden treasure inside is hid.

**161.** Alive without breath, as cold as death; never thirsty, ever drinking, All in mail [a type of body armor or shell] never clinking.

**162.** This thing all things devours: birds, beasts, trees, flowers; gnaws iron, bites steel; grinds hard stones to meal; slays king, ruins town, and beats high mountain down.

RIDDLES 163 AND 164 WERE WRITTEN BY LEWIS CARROLL.

**163.** Dreaming of apples on a wall, and dreaming often, dear, I dreamed that, if I counted all. How many would appear?
(HINT: THIS IS A CONUNDRUM-ENIGMA THAT PLAYS ON A WORD IN THE ACTUAL STATEMENT.)

**164.** John gave his brother James a box. About it there were many locks. James woke and said it gave him pain; so gave it back to John again. The box was not with lid supplied, yet caused two lids to open wide. And all these locks had never a key. What kind of box, then, could it be?

**165**. A riddle from *Harry Potter and the Goblet of Fire*: First think of the person who lives in disguise, who deals in secrets and tells naught but lies. Next tell me what's always the last thing to mend. The middle of middle and end of the end? . . . Which creature would you be unwilling to kiss?

RIDDLES 166 TO 177 ARE FROM *THE DARK TOWER* SERIES BY STEPHEN KING. NOTE THAT THESE ARE CLASSIC OR WELL-KNOWN RIDDLES THAT WE HAVE COME ACROSS IN PREVIOUS CHAPTERS, AND THAT KING INCORPORATED INTO HIS NARRATIVES.

**166**. What has four wheels and flies?

**167**. What can run but never walks, has a mouth but never talks, has a bed but never sleeps, has a head but never weeps?

**168**. No sooner spoken than broken. What is it?

**169**. Feed me and I live, give me to drink and I die. What am I?

**170**. I pass before the sun yet make no shadow. What am I?

**171**. Light as a feather, yet no man can hold it for long.

**172**. If you break me, I'll not stop working. If you can touch me, my work is done. If you lose me, you must find me with a ring soon after. What am I?

**173**. What may go up a chimney down, but cannot go down a chimney up?

**174**. We are very little creatures; all of us have different features. One of us in glass is set; one of us you'll find in jet. Another you may see in tin, and a fourth is boxed within. If the fifth you should pursue, it can never fly from you. What are we?

**175**. Where may you find roads without cars, forests without trees, and cities without houses?

**176**. I have a hundred legs but cannot stand, a long neck but no head; and I ease the maid's life. What am I?

**177**. Cannot be seen, cannot be felt, cannot be heard, cannot be smelt. It lies behind the stars and beneath the hills. Ends life and kills laughter. What is it?

**178.** In spring I look happy, decked in comely array. In summer more clothing I wear. When colder it grows, I fling off my clothes, and in winter quite naked appear.

**179.** Higher than a house, higher than a tree, oh, whatever can that be?

**180.** What has a face and two hands but no arms or legs?

**181.** It has a thumb and four fingers but is not alive. Pray tell me, what bizarre creature could that be?

**182.** It gets wetter as it dries. What is it?

**183.** It has been in existence for millions of years, but it is no more than a month old. What could it possibly be?

**184.** It has a neck, but no head. What strange creature could it be?

**185.** We all have it, and no one can lose it. What could that be?

**186.** Strangely it goes up but never comes back down. What could that be?

**187.** It belongs to you but, curiously, it is used more by others. What is it?

**188.** What kind of cheese is made backwards?

**189.** What can you catch but not throw?

**190.** What is full of holes but still holds water?

**191.** It looks like water, but it's an illusion. It sits on sand and lays on concrete. People have been known to follow it everywhere and get nowhere. All we can do is stare at it.

**192.** I am pronounced as one letter but written with three. I'm double and can come in black, blue, and gray. I read but need a brain to understand.

**193.** They can be harbored, but few hold water. They can be nursed, but only by holding them against someone else. We can carry them, but not with our arms. We can bury them, but not in the earth.

## CHAPTER 6

# THE RIDDLER'S LEGACY: RIDDLES IN POPULAR CULTURE

*"I am a man of few words, but many riddles."*

—FRANK GORSHIN (1933–2005)

Batman is one of the best-known comic book superheroes of all time, disguising himself as a rich socialite during the day, known as Bruce Wayne, and becoming a black-cloaked and -masked figure at night to fight crime in Gotham City. Batman was introduced in *Detective Comics'* issue No. 27 in May 1939, and was created by artists Bob Kane and Bill Finger. He is also known as The Caped Crusader, The Dark Knight, and the World's Greatest Detective. In each episode, Batman faces an archenemy who tries to outfight and outwit him. One of his enemies is the Riddler, a criminal mastermind who leaves Batman clues in the form of riddles and word games.

FRANK GORSHIN AS THE RIDDLER IN THE 1966 *BATMAN: THE MOVIE,* WITH CESAR ROMERO AS THE JOKER AND LEE MERIWETHER AS CATWOMAN.

He is Batman's most clever foe, who wears a question mark on his clothes and carries a cane in the shape of a question mark.

As a villain, the Riddler made his first appearance in a 1948 comic book. Here is an example of one of his riddles, which exhibits the style of a conundrum:

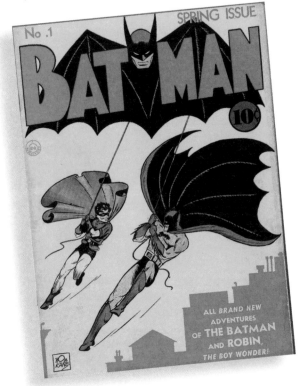

THE FIRST ISSUE OF *BATMAN* COMIC (SPRING 1940).

**194. What is the beginning of eternity, the end of time and space, the beginning of every end and the end of every race?**

The incorporation of riddles into comic books, television shows, and movies can be attributed to the legacy of the Riddler (the late actor Frank Gorshin most famously played the Riddler in various films). The evil character in the *Saw* movie series is one of the Riddler's descendants. His name, quite appropriately, is Jigsaw, and his captives must solve his riddles to save their lives (not unlike the Riddle of the Sphinx).

In one episode, the Riddler exclaimed, "Riddle me this!" This phrase is now a colloquial expression that entices us to provide an answer to a question that may not have an answer. And it may be the source for the spread of riddling across pop culture, from movies to video games and online. For example, the popular webcomic xkcd created in 2005 by American writer Randall Munroe often includes riddles—in true Riddler style—such as the following one:

**195. Hungry and angry are two words that end in "-gry." What's the third word in the English language?**

Recalling the nonsense riddles of Lewis Carroll, there is no third word. The answer to the riddle is actually "language." The first statement is a misdirection, and the answer is in the question: "What's the third word in the English language?" The third word in the phrase "the English language" is "language."

## *A Curious Thing*

In early versions of the superhero narrative, Batman is aided by his sidekick, Robin, along with his butler and the Batmobile. Robin and Batman are known as the Dynamic Duo. Robin first appeared as Dick Grayson in the April 1940 issue of *Detective Comics*. In the 1980s, Robin receded from the Batman narrative and became his own hero, Nightwing.

The Butler is Bruce Wayne's helper, who prepares him for his role as Batman by maintaining his wardrobe and the Batmobile. In one version, the latter has wing-shaped tailfins and is outfitted in armor with lasers, rockets, an on-board telephone, radar, dash monitor, computer, and police beacon. It can maneuver a quick 180° "bat-turn" due to the two rear-mounted parachutes and is equipped with a smoke emitter, a nail spreader, and a Batmobile Parachute Pickup Service Signal that picks up the Batmobile's parachute from the city street.

BURT WARD AS ROBIN AND ADAM WEST AS BATMAN IN THE 1966 *BATMAN: THE MOVIE.*

Online riddling has become rather widespread, including the riddle games *NotPron* and *Zahada*. *NotPron* was created in 2004 by German game developer David Münnich. Each level of difficulty is the basis for solving riddles at the next higher level. Most of the riddles are obscure, unless you start at the lowest level and work up. *Zahada*, which was developed by an anonymous creator, also provides levels, but unlike *NotPron*, the riddles are traditional ones.

And many role-playing video games (RPVGs) often include riddles, recalling ancient riddle games and the use of riddles in contests of bravery. From the latest version of *Dungeons & Dragons* to current RPVGs, riddling continues to be part of the story, no matter the medium in which it is delivered.

The board game Time's Up! is a charades-based game, published by R&R Games. Released in 1999, with recent editions, this popular game has sold millions of copies and is played with teams of two or more players in three rounds, just like mime charades.

Of course, long before the internet existed, television game shows based on riddling were very popular. In 1949, *Pantomime Quiz* aired in New York on CBS, running until August 1951. After that, other TV channels took it over, renaming it *Stump the Stars*, until the last episode aired in 1959 on ABC. The show had two teams of four contestants each (three celebrity regulars and one guest). In each round, one team member acted out a phrase or a name in the usual way, while the other three team members tried to guess it. Each team had five rounds. The team that took the least amount of time to guess the answer won the game.

Another charade game on syndicated television was *Celebrity Charades*, which debuted in January 1979, lasting until 2008. It was modeled after *Stump the Stars*, but each team had its own room in which to compete. One player from each team was sent to the stage to retrieve a phrase to be acted out in the players' room. When a member guessed the phrase correctly, that person was then sent out to the stage for another clue, and so on, until five phrases were guessed. The phrases concealed a hidden theme, and the first team to guess that theme won the game.

Although riddling now crisscrosses all mass media, it is undoubtedly in the realm of cinema that it has become somewhat of a staple, especially in the mystery and thriller genres. An example is the blockbuster adventure/heist movie *National Treasure* (2004), where the appeal and emotional pull of the narrative are embedded in cryptography and riddling. The protagonist, historian and code-breaker Benjamin Franklin Gates (Nicholas Cage)—whose name alludes to Benjamin Franklin, an expert cryptographer and riddle maker in his own time—is charged with finding a coded map that leads to the location of the national treasure. He figures out the map's location by answering the following riddle:

THE DECLARATION OF INDEPENDENCE PLAYS AN IMPORTANT ROLE IN THE MOVIE *NATIONAL TREASURE*.

THE PYRAMID AND EYE OF PROVIDENCE WERE LATE EIGHTEENTH-CENTURY SYMBOLS OF THE ILLUMINATI SECT OF BAVARIA.
THE ILLUMINATI ARE AT THE CENTER OF DAN BROWN'S NOVEL *ANGELS & DEMONS*.

**196. The legend writ, the stain affected. The key in Silence undetected. Fifty-five in iron pen, Mr. Matlock can't offend.**

The cipher used to make the map is an Ottendorf one, written in invisible ink on the back of the Declaration of Independence, which is the answer to this riddle, and the key is a detail within the map itself. The encrypted message is linked to the Silence Dogwood letters—letters written by Benjamin Franklin under this pen name. The message leads the investigators to the bell tower of Independence Hall, where they find a pair of glasses. When they use the glasses to read the back of the Declaration of Independence, a critical clue appears: "Here at the Wall." After a series of subsequent clues, the treasure is eventually located. The movie's narrative also includes secret societies, such as the Freemasons and the Knights Templar, adding to its atmosphere of conspiracy and mystery.

The riddle game plays a central role in the movie *Inside Man* (2006). A group of bank robbers seemingly executes the "perfect" robbery, but the situation goes awry when a hostage crisis develops, pitting the head detective against the ringleader. At one point during negotiations, the ringleader gives the detective a riddle to solve over the phone. As in any riddle game, if the police are unable to solve it, there will be dire consequences for the hostages. Here is the riddle:

**197. What weighs more, all the trains that pass through Grand Central Station in a year or all the trees cut down to print US currency?**

The answer—"they both weigh the same because they both weigh nothing"—rests on ingenious wordplay. Grand Central in New York City is not a "station" but a "terminal," so trains do not "pass through" it. The paper used to make money is not made from wood pulp but is composed of cotton and linen.

Many popular novels also include riddles that are intrinsic to their plots. In *The Grey King* (1975), the third book in *The Dark Is Rising* series by Susan Cooper, two of the main characters, Will and Bran, must win a riddle game in order for Bran to claim his heritage as the Pendragon. In Patricia A. McKillip's *The Riddle Master* trilogy (starting in 1976), "riddlery," or the ancient art of riddle making, is taught at the College of Caithard, based on books recovered from the ruins of the ancient School of Wizards. The riddles are constructed with three components—the Question, the Answer, and the Stricture (the limitation to a singular answer)—which reflect the dialectic structure of riddles. Evoking many of the ancient themes of riddling, this series brings the importance of riddles into contemporary focus by emphasizing that the wisdom of the ancients must not be lost if we are to avoid a catastrophic destruction of civilization.

As mentioned earlier, Dan Brown is an author who incorporates riddles and puzzles into the narratives of his bestselling novels, including *Angels & Demons* (2000), *The Da Vinci Code* (2003), and *Inferno* (2013). In *Angels & Demons*, the protagonist, Professor Robert Langdon, is immediately confronted with a riddle that he must solve in order to unravel the mysterious kidnapping of four cardinals and to stop the Illuminati from bombing the Vatican. Here's the riddle:

**198. FROM SANTI'S EARTHLY TOMB WITH DEMON'S HOLE. 'CROSS ROME THE MYSTIC ELEMENTS UNFOLD. THE PATH OF LIGHT IS LAID, THE SACRED TEST. LET ANGELS GUIDE YOU ON YOUR LOFTY QUEST.**

The riddle tells Langdon that he must follow the Path of Illumination, the answer to this riddle, to save the Catholic Church. The bomb is made of antimatter, stolen from CERN (European Organization for Nuclear Research) in Switzerland. The Path is a trail of four locations, called the Altars of Science, which lead to the Church of Illumination, the secret location of the Illuminati.

In the *Da Vinci Code*, Brown also tapped into people's love of riddles and secret codes as part of the mystery. The novel is about an enigmatic code, called the Da Vinci Code, which Langdon ultimately decodes, by interpreting the individual clues to its meaning scattered throughout the plot. To make his story as verisimilar as possible,

Brown introduced a neologism, "cryptex," to denote a portable cylinder where secret messages are hidden. He describes it as "five doughnut-sized disks of marble that had been stacked and affixed to one another within a delicate brass framework." The cylinder works like a combination lock, recalling the ancient scytales of Greek secret writing and reinforcing the novel's overall cryptographic style.

The use of riddles, puzzles, and cryptography in mystery fiction can be traced back to Edgar Allan Poe's short story "The Gold-Bug" (1843). Protagonist William Legrand is bitten by a gold-colored bug, and his servant fears, because of the bite, that Legrand may be losing his mind. On the throes of insanity, Legrand organizes a team to find a buried treasure whose location he discovered after deciphering a secret message. The decipherment of the message is the crux of the narrative. The cipher is a map containing a cryptogram, which, when unraveled, contains directions to the treasure that was buried by Captain Kidd. "The Gold-Bug" was an instant success, becoming Poe's most widely read work during his lifetime. It also helped popularize puzzles as key features of mystery stories. Below is the ciphertext in Poe's story that challenges the reader to decode it along with the protagonist.

This cipher is made with numbers and symbols that stand for letters. Using these clues can you decode this cipher? The start of the message is "A good glass in the bishop's hostel in the devil's seat forty-one degrees . . .":

**199.** 53‡‡†305))6*;4826)4‡.)4‡);
806*;48†8¶60))85;1‡(;:‡*8†83(88
)5*†;46(;88*96*?;8)*‡(;485);5*†2:
*‡(;4956*2(5*- 4)8¶8*;4069285);)
6†8)4‡‡;1(‡9;48081;8:8‡1;48†85;
4)485†528806*81(‡9;48;(88;4(‡?
34;48)4‡;161;:188;‡?;

The "bishop's hostel" is the site of an ancient manor house where the protagonist finds a narrow ledge resembling the outline of a chair (the "devil's seat"). Using a telescope with the given bearing, he spots a skull among the branches of a large tree through which a weight has to be dropped—the bug itself. From there, they locate the treasure with the cipher's directions.

Sir Arthur Conan Doyle also used cryptography in his Sherlock Holmes story "The Adventure of the Dancing Men" (1903). This story involves a cipher, which is introduced in the story when Mr. Hilton Cubitt of Ridling Thorpe Manor in Norfolk goes to consult Sherlock Holmes, giving him a ripped piece of paper with a mysterious sequence of stick figures:

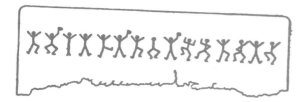

The code is a simple substitution cipher where each figure stands for a letter of the alphabet and a digit from 0 to 9.

In the Holmes story, this cryptogram is sent to Cubitt's young American wife, Elsie Patrick. Elsie had made her husband promise to never ask about her past. He swears to maintain his promise but still wonders what sinister warning the coded message might harbor. Holmes decides to take the case. The solution to the cryptogram, and others that Cubitt sends to Holmes, concerns a past secret, which comes back to haunt Elsie—her covert romance with an American gangster named Abe Slaney in Chicago. Cubitt would have most likely still loved his wife, despite her past. But keeping it a secret cost Elsie her husband in the end.

Today, riddles, ciphers, and codes are found throughout pop culture—on TV shows, in video games, in movies, in bestselling books, and so on. Clearly, our instinctual need for riddles has not dissipated in the morass of media and genres that are now available.It actually seems to thrive in a pop-culture environment.

# SOLVE THESE RIDDLES FROM POP CULTURE

(THE ANSWERS START ON PAGE 135)

RIDDLES 200 TO 210 ARE BY THE RIDDLER IN VARIOUS *BATMAN* TV
EPISODES. A FEW OF THESE ARE REPHRASINGS OF CLASSIC RIDDLES,
AND A FEW ARE TONGUE IN CHEEK.

**200.** Why is an orange like a bell?

**201.** What is always on its way here, but never arrives?

**202.** What won't run long without winding?

**203.** Why is a woman in love like a welder?

**204.** What has branches and leaves and no bark?

**205.** How many sides has a circle?

**206.** Which president wears the largest hat?

**207.** I have billions of eyes, yet I live in darkness. I have millions of ears, yet only four lobes. I have no muscle, yet I rule two hemispheres. What am I?

**208.** What kind of men are always above board?

**209.** If you look at the number on my face, you will not find thirteen anywhere.

**210.** The eight of us go forth and not back to protect the king from a foe's attack.

RIDDLES 211 TO 213 ARE FOUND IN MOVIES.

**211.** What is the air-speed velocity of an unladen swallow? What do you mean? An African or a European swallow? (*Monty Python and the Holy Grail*, 1975)

**212.** In my mind's eyes, I see three circles joined in priceless, graceful harmony. Two full as the moon, one hollow as a crown. Two from the sea, five fathoms down. One from the earth, deep under the ground. The whole, a mark of high renown. Tell me, what can it be? (*Clash of the Titans*, 1981: In the movie, Perseus, son of Zeus, is destined to marry Princess Andromeda. But the satyr Calibos is against it. Perseus sets out to defeat the malicious satyr and comes across this riddle on his journey.)

**213.** What's round, but not always around? It's light sometimes; it's dark sometimes. Everyone wants to walk all over me. What am I? (*Transporter 2*, 2005)

THE REMAINING RIDDLES ARE NOT FOUND IN ANY SPECIFIC POP-CULTURE REFERENCE, BUT THEY ARE POPULAR ON WEBSITES AND OTHER MEDIA. THEY HAVE BEEN REPHRASED OR ALTERED HERE SO THAT THEY CAN BE SOLVED WITHOUT RELYING ON PREVIOUS KNOWLEDGE. SOME OF THEM ARE TONGUE IN CHEEK.

**214**. It has a head and a tail but no legs. It can also be flipped. What is it?

**215**. There is a room that ghosts avoid because they do not belong in it. What room is that?

**216**. What can point in all directions—up, down, left, right—but cannot reach any destination by itself?

**217**. It has six faces, but cannot see. It has the shape of a cube. What is it?

**218**. Two monkeys are sitting in a tree. At a certain point, one jumps off. Why does the other monkey also jump off?

**219**. It runs around a yard, but it does not move. What could it possibly be?

**220**. I am dirty when I have white markings on me, and clean when I am black. What am I?

**221**. It can be cracked, told, and played. Some laugh at me, others do not. What am I?

**222**. I start in infancy and end when life is over. I can also be counted and celebrated. What am I?

**223**. It can travel anywhere in the world simply by staying in a corner. What is it?

**224**. I am round like a ball, but do not bounce. I shine only at night. What am I?

**225**. There is only one word that is spelled incorrectly in any dictionary. What is it?

**226**. If you take off my skin I will not cry, but you will. Who am I?

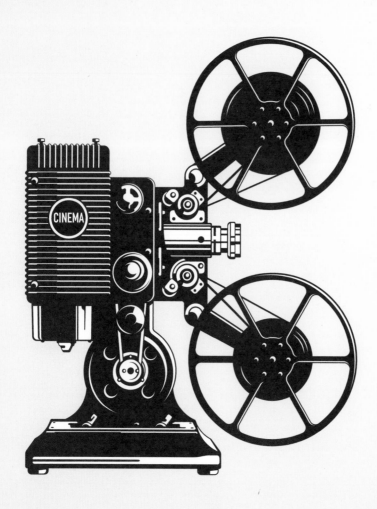

**227.** What lets you see right through a wall?

**228.** What side of a turkey has the most feathers?

**229.** What instrument can be enjoyed and heard, but not seen or touched?

**230.** What word becomes shorter when you add two letters to it?

**231.** The more you take, the more you leave behind. What could they possibly be?

**232.** If you throw a blue stone into the Red Sea, what will it become?

**233.** You can buy me to eat, but you will never eat me. What am I?

**234.** What never asks questions but is often answered?

**235.** What has four legs but cannot walk?

**236.** I am an odd number. Take away one letter and I become even. What number am I?

**237.** A boy was rushed to the hospital emergency room. The ER doctor saw the boy and said, "I cannot operate on this boy. He is my son." But the doctor was not the boy's father. How could that be?

**238.** I travel very slowly when gliding along the ground. Maybe my shell weighs me down. In your garden, I am found. What am I?

**239.** What stays where it is when it goes off?

## CHAPTER 7

# PICTOGRAPHIC ENIGMAS: REBUSES AS VISUAL RIDDLES

*"Life is a succession of lessons which must be lived to be understood. All is riddle, and the key to a riddle is another riddle."* —RALPH WALDO EMERSON (1803-1882)

The plausible connection between riddles, myths, and the birth of culture has been considered throughout this book. This implies that riddles and language are intertwined in their origins. If so, then spontaneous playfulness is at the root of human sapience, as the scholar Johan Huizinga claims in his book *Homo Ludens* (1938). The fact that there is no ancient culture without riddles is indirect evidence in support of this hypothesis. As such, riddles constitute a universal feature of human language—its ability to interpret reality cleverly, rather than just refer to it.

A JAPANESE WOODCUT DEPICTING A REBUS.

Riddles are born in a sense of the sacredness and mystery of things, as the Riddle of the Sphinx implies. Writing also started out as part of the sacred. The ancient Egyptians called their writing system "hieroglyphic" because they used it to record hymns and prayers, register the names and titles of individuals and deities, and record various community activities; "hieroglyphic" is a Greek version of the Egyptian term, deriving from *hieros*, "holy," and *glyphein*, "to carve." Most scripts were deemed to have sacred or mystical origins. For example, the Cretans attributed their writing system as a gift from Zeus, the Sumerians from Nabu (the god of literacy), the Egyptians from Thoth (the god of writing), the Greeks from Hermes, and the list goes on.

The earliest form of writing was pictographic, drawing pictures to represent objects. So intuitive and functional is pictography that it comes as little surprise to find that it has not disappeared from our alphabet-based world. The figures designating "male" and "female" on washrooms and the "no smoking" signs in public buildings are examples of modern-day pictographs. Emoji writing is also part of new pictography, which blends text with picture words. Indeed, the word "emoji" is Japanese, meaning "picture word," or 絵文字. According to *Merriam-Webster*, the "e" means "picture, drawing" and "moji" stands for "letter, character."

In the origin of language and writing, pictography and riddles share a lot of conceptual space. There are some puzzles that are essentially visual riddles, or pictographic enigmas, as they can be called. They are known as "rebuses," which are messages constructed and deciphered by replacing words, or parts of words, with pictures, signs, and letters. Here's an example:

240.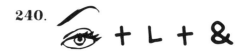

This is a rebus of the word "island." It's constructed with the pictograph of an eye (representing the letter "I" as a homophone), the letter "L," and the ampersand sign, which represents the word "and." When these signs are combined, we get the word "island."

As linguists and communications theorists have argued, writing systems are based on a so-called rebus principle, whereby a word or syllable is represented with a picture of an object whose name phonetically resembles the word or symbol in question, as the rebus above shows. Alphabets arose through the unconscious operation of this principle. For example, in the ancient Sumerian language, the pictograph for "arrow" was also used to represent "life." *Ti* is the word for "arrow," and *til* (nearly a homonym) is the word for "life." Because the concept of life was difficult to draw, someone at some point must have realized that the two words were virtually homonymous, and therefore used the same pictograph to represent the sound of the syllable "ti," irrespective of the meaning of the pictograph. Gradually, the sound became detached from pictographic representation and evolved into an independent

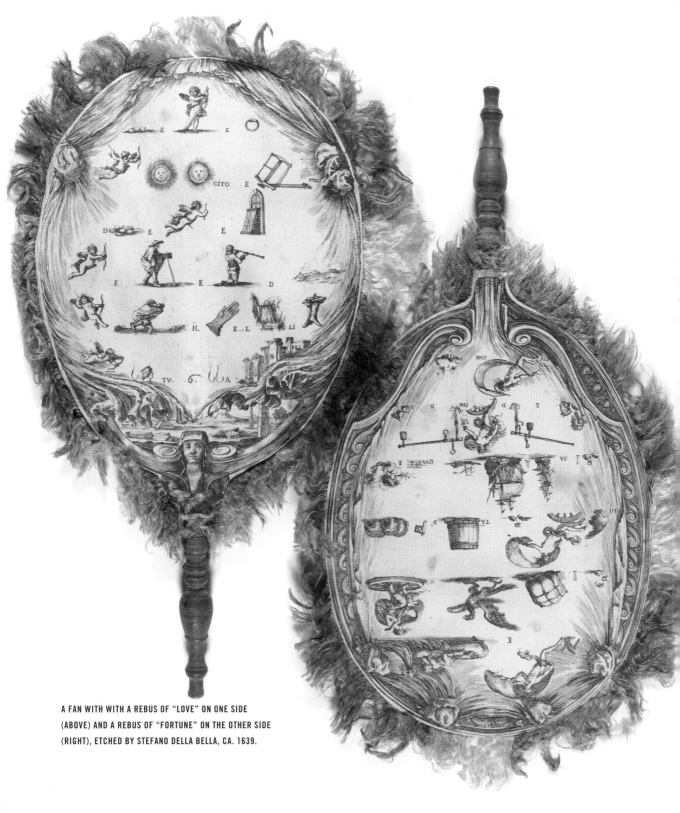

A FAN WITH WITH A REBUS OF "LOVE" ON ONE SIDE
(ABOVE) AND A REBUS OF "FORTUNE" ON THE OTHER SIDE
(RIGHT), ETCHED BY STEFANO DELLA BELLA, CA. 1639.

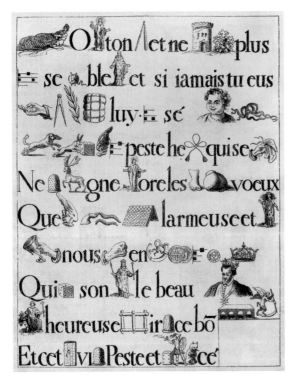

A REBUS FROM FRANCE, 1613.

sound unit, called a "phoneme," that could be used over and over in words.

Deciphering rebuses involves an interplay between concepts and their relation to words and their meanings. They are visual metaphors, corresponding to the metaphorical language of riddles—riddles evoke mental imagery through verbal metaphor, and rebuses do the same thing through visual metaphor. Rebuses have been a source of fascination throughout the world and across history. It is not known where, when, or why they originated, separate from the history of pictography and alphabets. Coins with rebuses inscribed on them, representing famous people or cities, were common in ancient Greece and Rome. During the Middle Ages, rebuses were frequently used to encode heraldic mottoes, alluding to the name of the bearer.

In Renaissance Italy, rebuses were employed both to communicate with people who did not read and to teach literacy. In the early part of the seventeenth century, the priests of the Picardy region of France put them on the pamphlets they printed for the Easter carnival, so that anyone— literate or not—could understand the message.

The word "rebus" in this sense was coined in the Picardy region in the early seventeenth century. It comes from the French *rébus*, derived from the Latin ablative plural of *res* ("thing"). It was first used to refer to satirical texts written as picture riddles where the words mean "picture things." It is not clear if rebuses developed into veritable puzzles as did riddles in the same era. There is some evidence, however, that they did. A French manuscript titled *Le premier livre des bigarrures où est traité de toutes sorties de folies* (*The First Book of Variegations in Which Is Discussed All Sorts of Follies*), by jurist and writer Étienne Tabourot (1584–1590), reveals that the puzzles in this collection also contain a significant number of rebuses.

Rebus writing spread during the subsequent seventeenth century. The German manuscript opposite is dated circa 1620. A close inspection of the text shows that the use of images is identical to how we use emojis in our text messages today—they stand for objects in the content of the message either to reinforce the word meaning or to illustrate it.

A GERMAN REBUS MANUSCRIPT, CA. 1620.

As this type of writing spread, it started to be used for profane and satirical purposes. As a result, authorities thought of it as subversive, thus banning many rebus texts. But the penchant for rebus materials could not be suppressed. They had become so popular throughout Europe that Ben Jonson (1572–1637), the English playwright and poet, trenchantly ridiculed them in his play *The Alchemist*.

By the eighteenth century, rebuses and riddles were combined as part of children's reading material. In 1788, American newspaper publisher Isaiah Thomas (1749–1831) published a children's Bible in Worcester, Massachusetts, that was partially based on rebus writing; Bible stories were retold with pictures to make the reading easier and more enjoyable for children. It was called, rather appropriately, *A Curious Hieroglyphic Bible*. Below is a page from that Bible.

Rebus cards also became popular in the same era, appearing for the first time in 1789.[28] They were in vogue in many parts of Europe,

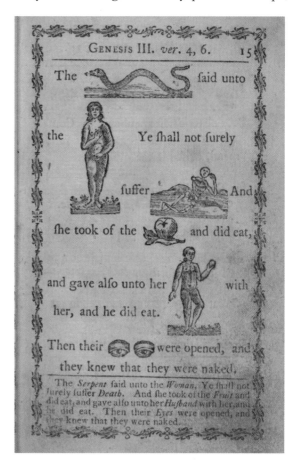

A PAGE FROM *A CURIOUS HIEROGLYPHIC BIBLE*, 1788.

MAY
I. C. U.
HOME?

40 Escort Cards,
85 designs for 10 cts

especially England and France. The escort card opposite dates to around 1870. It is deciphered as "May I see you home?"

The rebus was probably used as code to a loved one so that parents or guardians could not easily decipher it, much like how young people hide their messages today with various codes, including abbreviated writing and emojis. On the other hand, it may reflect a playful form of courtship based on challenging messages that were intended to display ingenuity, much like the riddle games of yore.

One of the most famous of all rebus cards was the one the king of Prussia, Frederick the Great (1712–1786), sent to the French satirist Voltaire (1694–1778) as an invitation to dinner, shown below.

This translates in French as *Deux mains* ("two hands") *sous* ("below") *p* (pronounced "pay" in French) *à* ("at") *cent* ("one hundred") *sous scie* ("below the saw"): that is, *Demain souper à Sanssouci?* ("Dinner tomorrow at Sanssouci?")

Voltaire answered the invitation with his own rebus: "G" for *Gé grand* and "a" for *a petit*. The result was *J'ai grand appétit* ("I have a great appetite").

Lewis Carroll became intrigued by rebuses as visual riddles. He sent a rebus to Georgina Watson, the daughter of George Watson, who was the postmaster of Merton College, Oxford.[29] The letter was sent on October 10, 1869, and its appearance is similar to today's emoji messages.

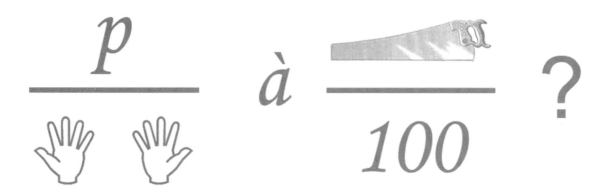

ABOVE: AN INTERPRETATION OF FREDERICK THE GREAT'S REBUS CARD TO VOLTAIRE. OPPOSITE: THE FRONT AND BACK OF AN ESCORT CARD, CA. 1870 (© LIBRARY COMPANY OF PHILADELPHIA).

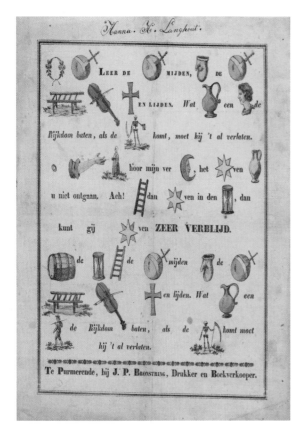

A DUTCH REBUS BY J. P. BRONSTRING, CA. 1830.

**241.**

X + Y + ☀

**242.**

🚗 + L + 🌴

The first one is the British poet Alfred, Lord Tennyson (1809–1892), and the second one is the Scottish philosopher Thomas Carlyle (1795–1881).

Combining pictographic with alphabetic symbolism, rebuses exemplify the power of human signs to encode meaning in various sensory modalities. A pictographic element may stand for its referent, the thing it depicts (the car above), or it may stand for the pronunciation of its referent's name (as the eye stands for the same pronunciation of the pronoun "I"). Rebuses remind us that we encode a large part of our knowledge about the world through visual symbols, not just written words. And like any riddle, they do not refer to something directly, but through association and imagination.

Rebuses have also become embedded in popular culture. In the United Kingdom, the game show *Catchphrase* (1986-2004) had contestants decipher partial phrases, much like rebuses. It actually started out on American television, but became more popular in England and then in Australia. Perhaps the American show *Concentration* (1958-1991) was the most famous of all TV

Today, rebuses have evolved into a genre of puzzle, although the rebus principle still appears in emoji and other types of visual writing. Like riddles, they have always been especially appealing to children. The following two are adapted from an 1865 issue of a popular nineteenth-century children's magazine, *Our Young Folks*.[30] They refer to two English writers (note that the "X" is to be read as the Roman numeral):

HOST HUGH DOWNS STANDING IN FRONT OF A *CONCENTRATION* GAME BOARD IN 1961.

game shows based on rebus puzzles. Matching pairs of cards were gradually removed from a board to reveal the parts of a rebus puzzle that contestants had to solve in order to win a match.

Rebus-based game shows are found in many parts of the world. There are now several websites that provide daily rebus puzzles or generate them on demand. Interestingly, the term "rebus" itself has become a metaphor for mystery, as can be seen in the series of *Inspector John Rebus* novels by Scottish writer Ian Rankin. The name of the detective protagonist is self-explanatory.

There are various types of rebus puzzles, but all are based on several substitution and layout techniques. A rebus puzzle might involve a play on the sound of letters or on their location in a string. The objective is to "read" the message out loud to see what it yields. A rebus that's comprised solely of letters, numbers, or symbols is called a "gramogram." Try to figure out what the following two rebuses say:

**243.** C U

**244.** W1111HILE

In the first example, the letters, when pronounced, are homophones of "see" and "you," hence the answer, "see you." This is known, more specifically, as a "phonogram." Together they make up a common expression. The same technique is used in writing text messages and other digital messages today. The second one is based on layout, in which letters and other symbols are laid out suggestively. We see several "1"s in the word "while." So, with some phonetic adjustment, we get the answer, "once in a while."

Many common rebuses are based on deciphering what message or phrase the juxtaposition of words suggests:

**245.** $\frac{\text{WATER}}{\text{BREATHE}}$

**246.** $\frac{\text{HEAD}}{\text{HEELS}}$

Rebuses that involve a combination of layout text and images are called "pictographic enigmas":

**247.**

**248.**

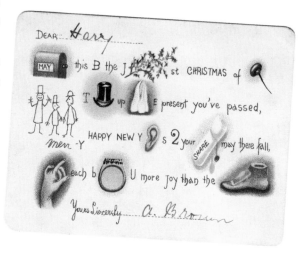

Like riddles, rebuses tap into a sense of language as a metaphorical code originating in wonder and the human need to grasp the world through images.

A HUMOROUS VICTORIAN HOLIDAY CARD IN A REBUS STYLE, CA. 1890.

# CONCLUSION

Originating at the dawn of civilization, riddles are among the oldest products of human ingenuity. Lewis Carroll claimed that he meant only nonsense with his riddles. But the type of nonsense to which Carroll alludes is the same that motivated the early orators and even philosophers. They are curious figments of the imagination, constituting playful experiments in thought and its connection to reality. Although this may be somewhat of a stretch, it is plausible that the ancients perceived riddles as providing bits and pieces of an "obscure code" to unlocking the meaning of the world—a sense that has not completely disappeared today. From the Riddle of the Sphinx to the everyday riddles we present to children, we sense unconsciously that each riddle might be a self-fulfilling prophecy. Everything is a riddle, until it is understood, including human beings. As Carroll himself so aptly put it in *Alice's Adventures in Wonderland*: " 'Who in the world am I? Ah, *that's* the great puzzle!'"

The "riddle instinct" is universal. All cultures have created riddles that are meant to shed light on things through metaphor, as well as to provide comic relief from the worries of everyday life. The Riddle of the Sphinx may well be humanity's first expression of the universal angst humans felt about being in the dark about the nature of life, as well as the problems of time and eternity. The Russian-born twentieth-century esotericist P. D. Ouspensky (1878–1947) perfectly sums it up in his book *A New Model of the Universe* (1931), when he says, "The problem of Eternity, of which the face of the Sphinx speaks, takes us into the realm of the impossible. Even the problem of Time is simple in comparison with the problem of Eternity."

# SOLVE THESE REBUSES

(THE ANSWERS START ON PAGE 137)

SOME OF THESE REBUSES ARE CLASSICS, BUT SEVERAL ARE NEW.

**249.** 4GETit

**250.** LIFE–LIFE

**251.**
HAbirdND is worth BU2SH

**252.** TIME–TIME

**253.** LIFE1111TIME

**254.** SPEAK–SPEAK

**255.**
THIS HAPPENS MILLI1110N
X X X X.

**256.**
[BAD–BAD] ABOUT WHAT
HAPPENED.

IT IS NOW
BRIDGE
WATER

**257.**
HISTORY–HISTORY–HISTORY
TIME––TIME.

**258.**
READ:
WRONG–WRONG ≠ RIGHT

**259.**
THEY LIVE ON

AN 👁 + 🏔 IN THE ☀

**260.**
 OF CITY–CITY

(HINT: THIS IS THE TITLE OF A CHARLES DICKENS NOVEL.)

**261.**
THIS IS [GOOD–GOOD]
TO 🐝 TRUE

**262.**
LIFE IS NOT A

 + + + EEEEE.

**263.**

 ON A HOT

(HINT: THIS IS THE TITLE OF A TENNESSEE WILLIAMS PLAY.)

**264.**

ON
___
WORLD

**265.**

LONG
___
DUE

**266.**

MEALinMEAL

**267.**

ON

**268.**

FUNNY FUNNY WORDS WORDS
WORDS WORDS

**269.**

ONCE
___
TIME

**270.**

HAI/RS

**271.**

2  / NOT 2

**272.**

GET
___
IT

**273.**

 ONLY HAVE 4 U

# RIDDLE ANSWERS

## FRONT AND BACK COVER

Front top: humans; front right: shadow; front bottom: newspaper; front left: schoolhouse; back top: sponge; back right: fleas; back bottom: hunger; back left: pride.

## INTRODUCTION

**1**. A smile.

## CHAPTER 1

**2**. Humans. They crawl on all fours as babies, then walk on two legs as grown-ups, and finally need a cane in old age to get around.

**3**. Same answer as above.

**4**. A young lion Samson had killed with his bare hands that had bees constructing a hive in its corpse. The lion is both "the eater" and "the strong"; the "sweetness" refers to the honey that the bees were producing inside the lion's body.

**5**. Fleas, or in some versions, lice.

**6**. Day and night.

**7**. A river? A rowboat? A sheep? A plough?

**8**. A weaving shuttle? A tool?

**9**. A rain cloud?

**10**. There is no known or singular answer to this riddle, although the allusion to some divinity is clearly implied.

**11**. This signifies one of the daughters of Lot, since the Bible recounts that Lot slept with his daughters incestuously.

**12**. A ship is made by "cutting off" wood from a tree.

**13**. A wick.

**14**. An ibis. Seven musical instruments could be made from its carcass.

**15**. A laugh. The meanings of "laugh" are metaphorical, as in "laugh in someone's face" (to show contempt for someone) and "laugh out of the other side of one's mouth" (to feel embarrassed after realizing one is wrong in feeling satisfaction about something).

**16**. Play. This is a double entendre of the word "play"—it can refer to engagement in physical activities for enjoyment and to a theatrical work.

**17**. A schoolhouse. Blindness and seeing are metaphors of intellect and knowledge or lack thereof ("He is blind to the truth"; "Seeing is believing";etc.) This riddle was discovered in 1960 by anthropologist E. L. Gordon (see bibliography).

**18**. A rain cloud. The rain inflates and expands a cloud, appearing "fat," metaphorically speaking. The analogy used in the riddle is between the gradual expansion of the cloud and that of a woman's stomach during pregnancy.

**19**. A human being. This is a version of the Riddle of the Sphinx.

**20**. A year with its months, days, and nights. Here are the metaphorical analogies: "father" = the year; "twelve children" = the months; "thirty daughters" = days in a typical month; "white" = days; and "black" = nights.

**21**. A cow. The riddle describes the anatomy of a cow (four teats, hooves, and so on) and what they allow the cow to do, such as "ward off dogs" (back hooves).

**22**. A year. This riddle, like number 20, alludes to the twelve months of the year ("a twelve-spoked wheel"), on which stand "720 sons of one birth" (360 days and 360 nights).

**23**. A coconut. A coconut "bears" water in an analogy to how a woman bears children, who survive in water (amniotic fluid) in the womb. It can also refer to a pregnant woman.

**24**. A bird.

**25**. A dog.

**26**. The sun—or more exactly, the lack of sunlight. Lotuses can grow in the shade, but they generally grow best in full sunlight.

**27**. Hope. Each suitor bears the hope of marrying the princess, asking her to marry him (at night), but being rejected at dawn. Of course, *love* could also satisfy the description of this riddle. It's ambiguous.

**28**. Blood. Blood is red and warm and flows like water, and blood is what runs through the veins like a flame when someone is in love.

**29**. Turandot. She is cold "like ice" toward her suitors, yet she herself "burns" inside with anger. Again, there may be other answers to this riddle, in general, but the story constrains the answer to Turandot.

**30.** A snake. Snakes "bunch" up in places like a "hummock" (a knoll or mound); they "curl" up "under a stone"; and they look like a curled disc near a tree "stump."

**31.** The stars. They belong to the night and "disappear" at daytime.

**32.** Tomorrow. Tomorrow is something that will always be and yet never was because when it does come, it's called "today."

**33.** A river. The metaphors are common ones for rivers—they "run," they "murmur," they have a "mouth" (where they debouch into another river, a lake, etc.), and they flow in a "[river]bed."

**34.** Silence.

**35.** Water.

**36.** The sky.

## CHAPTER 2

**37.** A mule. This allusive riddle refers to the mule as the offspring of a donkey and a horse (animals of "mingled race" and "of others am I born") and sterile ("none is born of me").

**38.** A reed. This riddle describes writing, and it is the second riddle in the collection of Symphosius. Reed material for writing was common in the era—it is a plant that grows in water ("sweet darling of the banks"). The riddle alludes to the fact that writing in the era was used mainly for poetry ("I sing for the Muses") and executed with black ink ("drenched with black"). As a substitution of oral speech ("the tongue's messenger"), writing is carried out by "guiding fingers pressed."

**39.** Writing or a writer.

**40.** Pyrrhos.

**41.** Liberality. Liberality is portrayed in the work as the highest refuge of virtue, gift of fame, truth of heaven, and source of true happiness. The riddles in this work require knowledge of the philosophical tenets behind Hinduism, even though their answers embody universal truths.

**42.** A dog companion.

**43.** The moon.

**44.** A comb. The solution to this riddle hinges on decoding the metaphorical meaning of "beast" as a device rather than an animal.

**45.** Hunger.

**46**. First, he goes across the river with the goat, leaving the wolf and cabbage alone with no dire consequences, seeing as wolves don't eat cabbage. On the other side of the river, he drops off the goat and comes back alone. When he gets back to the original side, he must decide between the wolf or the cabbage. Let's say he goes with the cabbage. He crosses the river with the cabbage, drops it off, and then goes back to the original side with the goat in tow (since the goat would eat the cabbage). Back on the original side, he drops off the goat and goes over to the other side with the wolf. He drops off the wolf with the cabbage and then travels back alone to pick up the goat. He rows to the other side with the goat, and then collecting all three—the goat, the wolf, and the cabbage—he continues on his journey.

**47**. An onion.

**48**. An eye.

**49**. An echo. The key clue is that an echo "will not speak," but will "answer him who speaks," since it is a reflection of sounds, including those made by the human voice. It cannot, by itself, be "pert in speech" or "rash of tongue," observing a principle of modesty, which in the medieval period was expected of "a modest maid."

**50**. A key. Keys open closed doors and guard a house for its master (keeping it locked).

Naturally, the master will guard the key, given its "great powers" to do the guarding with "little strength."

**51**. A hammer. A hammer's "body" (its handle) is not where it can "lay claim to strength," but rather its large "head," which can break things and strike someone or something forcefully in a "battle of heads."

**52**. A frog. A frog's "hoarse sounds" are its croaks, which it bellows from a pond ("the water's midst"). But given the hoarseness of the frog's "songs," no one will ever "praise them" as they would melodious ones.

**53**. A fox. This riddle is self-explanatory: a fox is "wise," "cunning," "keen-witted," and "versed in trickery."

**54**. A mirror. A mirror is a reflective surface that shows things that "it has seen before" (reflection) in the "radiant light." Mirrors come in all shapes ("No fixed form is mine").

**55**. A dream. A dream cannot be seen by the eyes because it takes place in the imagination. The characters in the dream speak and run, even if in real life they might do neither. The dream is not real in the physical sense, so, it is considered a "liar," but tells the truth nonetheless—a remarkable pre-Freudian riddle.

**56**. Courage. It is, indeed, the best weapon in times of danger.

**57**. The moon. The moon is connected to the "surf" (the tides); its phases occur in "rolling cycles," etc.

**58**. A bee. A bee is not born of "seed"; it makes honey from the nectar ("treasure") of flowers, which is then put on the "platters of kings," making them "yellow" in color. It bears "sharp spears of cruel war" (its stinger), which are "weapons."

**59**. A cat. This is self-explanatory. A cat is a "faithful vigilant guardian" who roams in the night through "unseeing shadows," using its keen eyesight to do so, staying away from dogs "who bark and bring cruel war" against it.

**60**. Water. Even before the Darwinian theory of evolution, this riddle asserts that animals such as birds and fish "once took their first life from me." Of course, this could also mean that these animals feasted on the water to assure their survival. Water "bears" (provides) sustenance to "forest oaks." The "slender needle" more than likely refers to the root of the tree, which draws water in, or else to a siphoning of the water for nourishment purposes.

**61**. The wind.

**62**. A shield. Shields were made from willow bark and cowhide in the era.

**63**. A cloud. A cloud is "multicolored" and has "rainy tears" (rain).

**64**. Lice.

**65**. An egg.

**66**. A thunderstorm.

**67**. Wine.

**68**. A shield.

**69**. An anchor.

**70**. A cart.

**71**. A candle.

**72**. A pen.

**73**. Humility.

**74**. Fire.

**75**. A needle.

**76**. A sponge.

**77**. Some kind of carrier; maybe a ship or a cart. Note the same kinds of objects and themes in many of the riddle collections of the era.

**78**. The wind.

## CHAPTER 3

**79**. Dew.

**80**. No more than one tail, if it is long enough.

**81**. Beauty.

**82**. Featherbeds.

**83**. Sheep, cows, and goats.

**84**. Sausages in casings ("entrails").

**85**. The snow is a "bird featherless" that lies in a "tree leafless," or bare tree, in winter. The sun, a "maiden speechless," causes the snow to melt, metaphorically eating the featherless bird.

**86**. A gravedigger.

**87**. Dividing up the camels in this manner would mean having to physically divide the camels, therefore killing them. So, Tartaglia suggested "borrowing an extra camel," for the sake of argument, not to mention humane reasons. Now with eighteen camels, he arrived at a practical solution: one heir was given one-half of eighteen camels (or nine camels), another one-third of eighteen (or six camels), and lastly, one-ninth of eighteen (or two camels). Nine camels plus six plus two more add up to the original seventeen. The extra camel could then be returned to its owner.

**88**. A bowl.

**89**. Only a stone's throw.

**90**. By his eyesight.

**91**. Because it cannot sit.

**92**. Boiling water.

**93**. None. Because straws do not have feet, so they cannot go anywhere.

**94**. Say one twice over.

**95**. Any musical instrument made of wood. Wood can be "dead," as in "deadwood," hence the peculiar phrasing of the riddle.

**96**. Shoemakers. Shoes are "worn out" as we walk in them and can often be "destroyed" to the delight of shoemakers, who can then make more.

**97**. Fear of poverty. Fear is evoked in a "hollow cave" and poverty is associated with "agitation," "toil," and "sweat."

**98**. Avarice. Those who suffer from greed will indeed pursue money and possessions with "solicitude" and "zeal," not realizing that money is the root of all evil.

**99**. Dreaming. The characters in a dream "walk" but do not move physically; they "speak" to other dream characters, "who are absent" physically and "hear" the latter.

**100**. House flies. House flies undergo a metamorphosis, ending up as "winged creatures"; they are pests who "attack other men," feasting on "their food even from their hands and tables."

**101**. Gold. In this casket made of gold, there is a skull with a manuscript in the eye. The inscription says that not everything that glitters is gold, warning us that we may desire gold foolishly.

**102**. Silver. This one is made of silver and has a picture of a blinking fool with an inscription that says the person who chooses silver is chasing something too elusive.

**103**. Lead. The final casket, made of lead, is the correct casket. It has a portrait of Portia and a scroll that says, "You that choose not by the view, chance as fair and choose as true."

**104**. A thorn (caught on a foot).

**105**. A windmill. Windmills were vital in the era these riddles were composed. They have "wings" (blades) on high, which of course do not enable it to fly. These "often move around," but the windmill itself stays in "the self-same spot." A windmill grinds grain into flour before men "can be fed" (with bread, of course).

**106**. A cuckoo. It is made of wood and is often "compared to foolish persons."

**107**. A question.

## CHAPTER 4

**108**. Time. Describing time metaphorically as "long," "short," "swift," "slow," "divisible," "extended," etc. is so common in everyday discourse that we often forget that these expressions tell us nothing about the physical nature of time—but rather propose strategies for envisioning time as a physical entity. Voltaire's riddle impels us to think abstractly about time.

**109**. A gadfly. The first line of the riddle plays on the meaning of the word "gad," which means "to move about by rambling." The second line plays on the dual meanings of the verb "fly," which means "to flee or retreat from something" and "a dipterous insect." The subsequent line completes the description of the gadfly as an irritating insect.

**110**. Hem-lock (hemlock). Jane Austen sees an extreme remedy to a woman's plight.

**111**. An actor.

**112**. Birdlime (an adhesive substance for trapping birds). The first part refers to the "music sweet" that is associated with the song of a "bird," and the next one plays on the meaning of "lime" as "manure for the ground." The final part defines "birdlime" as a "snare."

**113**. Cares – caress. "Cares" are "bitter." Add an "s" to get "caress," which is "sweet."

**114**. Today. Before its "birth," today does indeed have a different name—"tomorrow." For example, if "today" is Monday, then from the perspective of the day before, Sunday, it is labeled "tomorrow." And when it is "laid within the tomb," that is, when it is over, it takes a new name, "yesterday"—when Tuesday comes about, Monday is over, and we refer to it as "yesterday." Finally, though it lasts only one day, it changes its name three days in a row ("three days together") from "yesterday" to "today" to "tomorrow."

**115**. A, E, I, O, U. The vowel A is in "glass," E in "jet," I in "tin," O in "box," and U in "pursue" and "you." This exact same enigma is now found throughout riddle culture, retaining its popularity.

**116**. A watering pot.

**117**. A newspaper.

**118**. Pride. In this case, the word "swallow" can refer to different things, as exemplified in the expressions "He had to swallow his pride" and "Pride can swallow you up."

**119**. The cold, which freezes the water under bridges.

**120**. Mosquitoes. As explained by Benjamin Franklin in the 1737 edition of *Poor Richard's Almanack*: "The Army which it was said would land in Virginia, Maryland, and the Lower Counties on Delaware were not Musketers with Guns on their Shoulders as some expected; but their Namesakes, in Pronunciation, tho' truly spelt Moschitos, armed only with a sharp Sting . . . being bred in the Water; and therefore may properly be said to land before they become generally troublesome."

**121.**

## HEAD

heal (Change "**D**" to "**L**")

teal  (Change "**H**" to "**T**")

tell (Change "**A**" to "**L**")

tall (Change "**E**" to "**A**")

**TAIL** (Change "**L**" to "**I**")

**122.** Matchless. "Match" = eligible equally for marriage; "less" = inferior; matchless means "incomparable."

**123.** Friendship. "Friend" = someone who is always there; "ship" = a large vessel; friendship is defined as a "close relationship."

**124.** Baseball. "Base" = foundation; "ball" = round object; "Babe Ruth" was one of the greatest baseball players of all time.

**125.** Overlap. "Over" = things higher; "lap" = somewhere where one might sit; overlap refers to "events or things that occur simultaneously."

**126.** Dovetail. "Dove" = delicate bird; "tail" = hindmost part; dovetail refers to how things "can fit together" easily or conveniently.

**127.** Masterpiece. "Master" = someone who exerts dominance; "piece" = a portion; "masterpiece" is "something outstanding."

**128.** Showcase. "Show" = a spectacle; "case" = an instance; showcase means to exhibit things.

**129.** Warehouse. "Ware" = pottery; "house" = habitation; a warehouse is where things can be stored.

**130.** Woman. "Woe" = affliction; "man" = whole (term referring to humans in general); a woman, according to Austen, is the best "antidote" to affliction because she softens and heals.

**131.** Courtship (wooing). "Court" = wealth and pomp of kings; "ship" = monarch of the seas; courtship is described by Austen in terms of the power relations between the sexes, over which women reign.

**132.** Mississippi. The play is on "eye" as a homophone of "I."

**133.** Feat – feet.

**134**. Eye, which is a homophone of "I," like in number 132. The "eye of the storm" is the calm zone at the center of a storm, and the "eye of the wind" is the direction from which the wind is blowing.

**135**. Hat – ham.

**136**. Red – read.

**137**. Egg. To have "egg on your face" means that you appear foolish; the riddle is "Which came first, the chicken or the egg?"

**138**. Gloves. Wearing gloves protects "against the cold"; to "take them [gloves] off" means that we are ready to engage someone in a fight.

**139**. Lips. To "smack one's lips" conveys satisfaction; to "curl one's lip" indicates contempt.

**140**. Goose. To be on a "wild goose chase" means to be foolishly pursuing something unattainable.

**141**. Rainbow. "Chasing a rainbow" means pursuing an illusory goal.

**142**. Heat – heart.

**143**. Ice: To "break the ice" refers to doing or saying something to relieve tension, especially when people meet for the first time.

**144**. Iceberg. The "tip of the iceberg" refers to the small part of a much larger problem that remains hidden.

**145**. Bucket. To "kick the bucket" means to die.

**146**. Cake. A "piece of cake" refers to something that can be achieved easily.

**147**. Potato. A "hot potato" is a controversial issue.

**148**. Straws. The "last straw" is a further difficulty that makes a situation unbearable.

**149**. Cut – cat.

## CHAPTER 5

**150**. Only one person was "going to" St. Ives— the narrator of the rhyme.

**151**. A mountain. This riddle describes features of mountains that may escape attention, depicting them in a metaphorical way and poetically connecting images.

**152**. Wind. This riddle depicts and blends the sensory experiences associated with the wind.

**153**. Trust.

**154**. The fox burying his grandmother under a holly bush. This is not really an answer, but rather a play on the riddle form itself. It is a riddle about riddles, perhaps taking its cue from Lewis Carroll's Mad Hatter riddle.

**155**. A mirror. The image of a fire in the mirror does not mean that the looker is also on fire.

**156**. A death mask.

**157**. Teeth. The "red hill" refers to the gums, and of course, teeth (thirty) allow us to "champ" and "stamp" (crush), although they "stand still."

**158**. The sun, shining on daisies.

**159**. Darkness.

**160**. An egg.

**161**. Fish.

**162**. Time.

**163**. Ten. The answer is revealed by separating "often" into "of" and "ten."

**164**. Blow [box] to each other's head. "Locks" refers to the hair on the head; "lid" is used with the meaning of "eyelid."

**165**. A spider. This is a play on the first syllable. The clues appear to allude to a "spy," which is a homophone of the "spi" in spider. Here's how this is explained in the novel: "The sound often heard in the search for a hard-to-find word . . . A creature I wouldn't want to kiss . . . a spider!"

**166**. A garbage truck. A garbage truck, bearing garbage, attracts flies.

**167**. A river.

**168**. Silence.

**169**. Fire.

**170**. The wind.

**171**. Breath.

**172**. A human heart.

**173**. An umbrella.

**174**. See the answer to riddle 115.

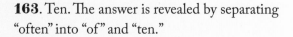

**175**. A map.

**176**. A broom.

**177**. The dark.

**178**. A tree. The tree's "clothing" consists of leaves.

**179**. A star.

**180**. A clock.

**181**. A glove.

**182**. A towel.

**183**. The moon.

**184**. A bottle.

**185**. A shadow.

**186**. Your age.

**187**. Your name.

**188**. Edam. This is the word "made" spelled backward.

**189**. A cold. "To catch a cold" means to suffer from it.

**190**. A sponge.

**191**. A mirage.

**192**. Eye. "Eye" is pronounced as one letter, "I." Eyes can be black, blue, and gray. And of course, we use eyes to read, but we need a brain to understand what we are reading.

**193**. Grudges.

## CHAPTER 6

**194**. The letter "e."

**195**. Language. Recalling the nonsense riddles of Lewis Carroll, there is no third word. The first statement is a misdirection, and the answer is in the question: "What's the third word in the English language?" The third word in the phrase "the English language" is "language."

**196**. The Declaration of Independence.

**197**. They both weigh the same because they both weigh nothing.

**198**. The Path to Illumination.

**199.** A good glass in the bishop's hostel in the devil's seat forty-one degrees and thirteen minutes northeast and by north main branch seventh limb east side shoot from the left eye of the death's-head a beeline from the tree through the shot fifty feet out. 5 = A, G = 3, ‡ = O, etc.

**200.** Both need to be peeled. A "peal of bells" is a loud ringing of bells and "peel" is a homophone of "peal."

**201.** Tomorrow.

**202.** A river.

**203.** They both carry a torch.

**204.** A library.

**205.** The inside and the outside.

**206.** The one with the largest head.

**207.** The human brain.

**208.** Chessmen.

**209.** A clock.

**210.** Chess pawns.

**211.** This riddle is a trick, as can be expected in a Monty Python movie. There is no answer.

**212.** A ring, which contains pearls in a circle of gold.

**213.** The moon.

**214.** A common coin.

**215.** The "living" room.

**216.** A finger.

**217.** A die (singular of dice).

**218.** "Monkey see, monkey do" (colloquial expression).

**219.** A fence.

**220.** A blackboard.

**221.** A joke.

**222.** Age.

**223.** A postage stamp.

**224.** The moon.

**225.** Incorrectly.

**226**. An onion.

**227**. A window.

**228**. The outside.

**229**. The voice.

**230**. Short.

**231**. Footsteps.

**232**. Wet.

**233**. A plate.

**234**. A doorbell.

**235**. A table.

**236**. Seven. Take away the "s" and the word becomes "even."

**237**. The doctor was his mother.

**238**. A snail.

**239**. An alarm clock.

## CHAPTER 7

**240**. Island.

**241**. Tennyson (Alfred, Lord Tennyson).

**242**. Carlyle (Thomas Carlyle).

**243**. See you.

**244**. Once in a while.

**245**. Breathe under water.

**246**. Head over heels.

**247**. Betrayal is a stab in the back.

**248**. *Of Mice and Men.*

**249**. Forget it.

**250**. Double life.

**251**. A bird in the hand is worth two in the bush.

**252**. Time after time.

**253**. Once in a lifetime.

**254**. Doublespeak.

**255**. This happens once in a million times.

**256**. Too bad about what happened. It is now water under the bridge.

**257**. History repeats itself, time after time.

**258**. Read between the lines: two wrongs do not make a right.

**259**. They live on an island in the sun.

**260**. *A Tale of Two Cities.*

**261**. This is too good to be true.

**262**. Life is not a bowl of cherries. "Bow" + "love" (symbolized by the heart) = "bowl of" (if pronounced rapidly).

**263**. *Cat on a Hot Tin Roof.*

**264**. On top of the world.

**265**. Long overdue.

**266**. In between meals.

**267**. On top of the world.

**268**. Too funny for words.

**269**. Once upon a time.

**270**. Splitting hairs.

**271**. To be or not to be.

**272**. Get over it.

**273**. I only have eyes for you.

# NOTES

## CHAPTER 1

**1**. GROTJAHN, MARTIN, *Beyond Laughter: Humor and the Subconscious* (New York: McGraw-Hill, 1966), 84.

**2**. TAYLOR, ARCHER, *The Literary Riddle before 1600* (Berkeley: University of California Press, 1948).

**3**. LASSNER, JACOB, *Demonizing the Queen of Sheba: Boundaries of Gender and Culture in Postbiblical Judaism and Medieval Islam* (Chicago: University of Chicago Press, 1993), 162.

**4**. WELLS, DAVID, *The Penguin Book of Curious and Interesting Puzzles* (Harmondsworth: Penguin, 1995), 169.

**5**. IBID.

**6**. IBID.

**7**. HOVANEC, HELENE, *The Puzzlers' Paradise: From the Garden of Eden to the Computer Age* (New York: Paddington Press, 1978), 10.

**8**. ARISTOTLE, *The Works of Aristotle, Vol. II* (Oxford: Clarendon Press, 1952), 5.

**9**. HUIZINGA, JOHAN, *Homo Ludens: A Study of the Play-Element in Human Culture* (New York: Beacon Press, 1938).

**10**. KÖNGÄS-MARANDA, ELLI, "Riddles and Riddling: An Introduction," *The Journal of American Folklore*, 89 (1976), 127–37.

**11**. AARNE, ANTTI, *Vergleichende Rätselforschungen* 3 vols. (Helsinki: Suomalainen Tiedeakatemia, 1918), 12.

**12**.TAYLOR, ARCHER, *The Literary Riddle before 1600* (Berkeley: University of California Press, 1948).

**13**. IBID.

**14**. KAIVOLA-BREGENHØJ, ANNIKKI, *Riddles: Perspectives on the Use, Function and Change in a Folklore Genre*, Studia Fennica Folkloristica 10 (Helsinki: Finnish Literature Society, 2001).

## CHAPTER 2

**15**. HOVANEC, HELENE, *The Puzzlers' Paradise: From the Garden of Eden to the Computer Age* (New York: Paddington Press, 1978), 14–5.

16. IBID.

17. SEBO, ERIN, "Was Symphosius an African? A Contextualizing Note on Two Textual Clues in the *Aenigmata Symphosii*," *Notes and Queries*, 56 (2009), 324–26.

18. SORRELL, PAUL, "Alcuin's 'Comb' Riddle," Neophilologicus, 80 (1996), 311–18.

19. IBID.

20. HOVANEC, HELENE, *The Puzzlers' Paradise: From the Garden of Eden to the Computer Age* (New York: Paddington Press, 1978), 22.

## CHAPTER 3

21. MCLUHAN, MARSHALL, *The Gutenberg Galaxy: The Making of Typographic Man* (Toronto: University of Toronto Press, 1962).

## CHAPTER 4

22. HOVANEC, HELENE, *The Puzzlers' Paradise: From the Garden of Eden to the Computer Age* (New York: Paddington Press, 1978).

23. IBID.

24. CHIARO, DELIA, *The Language of Jokes: Analysing Verbal Play* (London: Routledge, 1992).

## CHAPTER 5

25. DURKHEIM, EMILE, *The Elementary Forms of Religious Life* (New York: Collier, 1912), 12.

26. BOMBAUGH, CHARLES C., *Oddities and Curiosities of Words and Literature* (New York: Dover, 1962), 326.

27. COSTELLO, MATTHEW, J., *The Greatest Puzzles of All Time* (New York: Dover, 1988), 5.

## CHAPTER 7

28. COSTELLO, MATTHEW, J., *The Greatest Puzzles of All Time* (New York: Dover, 1988), 8.

29. COHEN, MORTON N., *The Letters of Lewis Carroll* (New York: Oxford University Press, 1979).

30. HOVANEC, HELENE, *The Puzzlers' Paradise: From the Garden of Eden to the Computer Age* (New York: Paddington Press, 1978), 68.

# BIBLIOGRAPHY

AARNE, ANTII. *Vergleichende Rätselforschungen* 3 vols. Helsinki: Suomalainen Tiedeakatemia, 1918.

ARISTOTLE. *The Works of Aristotle, Vol. II.* Oxford: Clarendon Press, 1952.

AUGARDE, TONY. *Oxford Guide to Word Games.* Oxford: Oxford University Press, 2003.

BOMBAUGH, CHARLES C. *Oddities and Curiosities of Words and Literature.* New York: Dover, 1962.

BORGMAN, DIMITRI. *Language on Vacation.* New York: Scribner's, 1965.

CARROLL, LEWIS. *Pillow Problems and a Tangled Tale.* New York: Dover, 1880.

CARROLL, LEWIS, AND MARTIN GARDNER. *More Annotated Alice: Alice's Adventures in Wonderland and Through the Looking-Glass.* New York: Random House, 1990.

CHIARO, DELIA. *The Language of Jokes: Analysing Verbal Play.* London: Routledge, 1992.

COHEN, MORTON N. *The Letters of Lewis Carroll.* New York: Oxford University Press, 1979.

COOK, ELEANOR. *Enigmas and Riddles in Literature.* Cambridge: Cambridge University Press, 2009.

COSTELLO, MATTHEW, J. *The Greatest Puzzles of All Time.* New York: Dover, 1988.

DOODY, MARGARET. *Jane Austen's Names: Riddles, Persons, Places.* Chicago: University of Chicago Press, 2015.

DURKHEIM, EMILE. *The Elementary Forms of Religious Life.* New York: Collier, 1912.

FREUD, SIGMUND. *Introductory Lectures on Psychoanalysis.* Digireads.com, 2013.

FUTSIS, STEFAN. *Word Freak.* Boston: Houghton Mifflin, 2001.

GORDON, EDMUND I. "A New Look at the Wisdom of Sumer and Akkad." *Bibliotheca Orientalis*, 17 (1960), 122–152.

GROTJAHN, MARTIN. *Beyond Laughter: Humor and the Subconscious.* New York: McGraw-Hill, 1966.

HASAN-ROKEM, GALIT AND SHULMAN, DAVID. *Untying the Knot: On Riddles and Other Enigmatic Modes*. Oxford: Oxford University Press, 1996.

HOVANEC, HELENE. *The Puzzlers' Paradise: From the Garden of Eden to the Computer Age*. New York: Paddington Press, 1978.

HUIZINGA, JOHAN. *Homo Ludens: A Study of the Play-Element in Human Culture*. New York: Beacon Press, 1938.

HUXLEY, FRANCIS. *The Raven and the Writing Desk*. New York: Harper and Row, 1976.

JUNG, CARL G. *The Essential Jung*. Princeton: Princeton University Press, 1983.

———. *Synchronicity: An Acausal Connecting Principle*. Routledge and Kegan Paul, 1972.

KAIVOLA-BREGENHØJ, ANNIKKI. *Riddles: Perspectives on the Use, Function and Change in a Folklore Genre*. Studia Fennica Folkloristica 10. Helsinki: Finnish Literature Society, 2001.

KÖNGÄS-MARANDA, ELLI. "Riddles and Riddling: An Introduction." *The Journal of American Folklore*, 89 (1976), 127–37.

LASSNER, JACOB. *Demonizing the Queen of Sheba: Boundaries of Gender and Culture in Postbiblical Judaism and Medieval Islam*. Chicago: University of Chicago Press, 1993.

LAUAND, JEAN. "The Role of Riddles in Medieval Education." *Revista Internacional d'Humanitats*, 16 (2009), 5–12.

LEARY, T. J. *Symphosius: The Aenigmata: An Introduction, Text and Commentary*. London: Bloomsbury, 2014.

LOYD, SAM. *Cyclopedia of 5000 Puzzles, Tricks, and Conundrums with Answers*. New York: Dover, 1914.

MCLUHAN, MARSHALL. *The Gutenberg Galaxy: The Making of Typographic Man*. Toronto: University of Toronto Press, 1962.

OLIVASTRO, DOMINIC. *Ancient Puzzles: Classic Brainteasers and Other Timeless Mathematical Games of the Last 10 Centuries*. New York: Bantam, 1993.

OLSHER, DEAN. *From Square One: A Meditation, with Digressions on Crosswords*. New York: Simon and Schuster, 2009.

RUSSELL, KEN AND PHILIP CARTER. *The Complete Guide to Word Games and Word Play*. London: Foulsham, 1995.

SCOTT, CHARLES T. *Persian and Arabic Riddles: A Language-Centered Approach to Genre Definition*. The Hague: Mouton, 1965.

SEBO, ERIN. "Was Symphosius an African? A Contextualizing Note on Two Textual Clues in the *Aenigmata Symphosii*." *Notes and Queries*, 56 (2009), 324–26.

SEYED-GOHRAB, A. A. *Courtly Riddles: Enigmatic Embellishments in Early Persian Poetry*. Leiden: Leiden University Press, 2010.

SORRELL, PAUL. "Alcuin's 'Comb' Riddle." *Neophilologicus*, 80 (1996), 311–18.

TAYLOR, ARCHER. *English Riddles from Oral Tradition*. Berkeley: University of California Press, 1951.

———. *The Literary Riddle Before 1600*. Berkeley: University of California Press, 1948.

University of Exeter. "Daily Crosswords Linked to Sharper Brain in Later Life." *Science Daily*, July 2019.

WELLS, DAVID. *The Penguin Book of Curious and Interesting Puzzles*. Harmondsworth: Penguin, 1992.

# IMAGE CREDITS

# INDEX

## ACKNOWLEDGMENTS

I would like to thank everyone at the Quarto Group who made this book possible, including my wonderful editor, Erin Canning, who not only approached me to write this book, but who has also transformed it into a literary magnum opus, with her keen editing and many apt suggestions. Needless to say, any infelicities that it may contain are my sole responsibility. I also must thank all the students who have taken the course on puzzle history I teach at the university; they have constantly inspired me and have always provided constructive criticism.

## ABOUT THE AUTHOR

Marcel Danesi, PhD, is a full professor of linguistic anthropology and the director of the program in semiotics at the University of Toronto. He is also co-director of the CogSci Network of the Fields Institute for Research in Mathematical Sciences. He has written extensively on puzzles, including *The Anthropology of Puzzles* (Bloomsbury, 2018) and *Ahmes' Legacy: Puzzles and the Mathematical Mind* (Springer, 2018). He also writes a puzzle blog for *Psychology Today* and composes puzzles for various magazines, including *Prevention* and *Reader's Digest*.